The Jewish Role in American Life

An Annual Review

The Jewish Role in American Life

An Annual Review

Volume 3

Editors
Barry Glassner
Hilary Taub Lachoff

Contributing Authors
Ted Merwin
Adam Rovner
Michael Staub
Nomi Stolzenberg
Meredith Woocher

USC Casden Institute for the Study of the Jewish Role in American Life
Los Angeles

ISBN 0-9717400-2-X

Book design by John Banner.
Set in Times New Roman.
Printed on Cascade 60 lb. offset.

Printed in the United States of America by
Delta, Incorporated, Valencia, California.

Published by the USC Casden Institute for the Study of the
Jewish Role in American Life
University of Southern California,
Grace Ford Salvatori Hall, Room 304,
Los Angeles, California 90089-1697

Contents

Acknowledgements

This volume represents the collaborative efforts of many people, over many months. We would like to expressly thank a few of these individuals, without whom this project would not have been possible. First, we'd like to thank Alan Casden for his generous support of this publication and the Casden Institute for the Study of the Jewish Role in American Life. We also thank the members of the Casden Institute Advisory Board, many of whom were founding members, and all of whom advise and support the Casden Institute in each of our efforts. They are: Lewis Barth, Mark Benjamin, Joseph Bentley, Alan Berlin, Jonathan Brandler, Michael Diamond, Solomon Golomb, Jonathan Klein, Ray Kurtzman, Susan Laemmle, Frank Maas, Gabriana Marks, Beth Meyerowitz, Michael Renov, Cara Robertson, Chip Robertson, Carol Brennglass Spinner, Scott Stone, Bradley Tabach-Bank, Ruth Weisberg, and Ruth Ziegler. We'd like to thank the University of Southern California, USC President Steven B. Sample, Provost Lloyd Armstrong and Joseph Aoun, Dean of the USC College of Letters, Arts and Sciences for their continued support and for providing the intellectual and cultural environment in which we thrive. Our thanks and congratulations to each of the contributors to this volume; we are proud to be able to publish your work. Finally, thanks to Diane Krieger for exemplary editing, proofreading, and assistance with the Introduction, Susan Wilcox for Development operations, and USC Senior Vice President Martha Harris for editorial suggestions.

Introduction

By Barry Glassner, Diane Krieger and Hilary Taub Lachoff

It is a truism to say that the American-Jewish community has played a vital role in shaping the politics, culture, commerce and multi-ethnic character of life in the United States. Yet most academic programs focus solely or primarily on the religious or historical study of American Jewry. USC's Casden Institute for the Study of the Jewish Role in American Life is unique in that it studies contemporary issues of Jewish life in the United States, with a particular emphasis on the West. The Jewish perspective and experience have influenced the region in countless ways: Jewish entrepreneurs like Levi Strauss were among the first to venture out West; Hollywood and much of the entertainment industry were born soon thereafter, identifiably the offspring of Jewish parentage; and while Jewish demographics are in decline in traditional centers of American Jewish life, namely the East and the Midwest, the Jewish population in the West since the 1970s has more that tripled. As of 2000, California ranked second only to New York in terms of Jewish statewide population, with Florida a distant third.

Understandably, the appetite for a better understanding of Jewish identity is palpable in the American West. We see it in the rising tide of adult *B'nai Mitzvah* ceremonies and ritual conversions, in the kaleidoscope of races and ethnicities among children attending Jewish Sunday schools; in the proliferation of campus Hillels; in the re-invigoration of progressive Jewish movements akin to the Workman's Circle of earlier decades and newer secular groups, such as the Culver City-based Sholem Community, emphasizing Yiddish language preservation and re-interpretation of Jewish ritual. This multifaceted rise in Jewish awareness attests to a lingering desire for Jewish connectedness in the West quite apart from being mindful of God's *mitzvot*.

Since its founding in 1998, the Casden Institute has hosted dozens of conferences, lectures and special events exploring what American Jews are thinking, saying, studying, doing and publishing. As part of that mission, each year the institute publishes an annual review. Now in its third year, this volume of scholarly essays takes a thematic approach to five key areas: values, culture, image, politics and education. Specifically, the 2004 edition considers the various ways in which, over the past century, the struggle for Jewish inclusion in American life seems to have shifted to a struggle *against* Jewish assimilation. In areas of popular culture, particularly in comedy and in theater, contributors to this volume argue that Jewish influences have suffused the mainstream to the point that they now constitute American archetypes. However, in areas of social policies and practices – such as divorce law, religious education and political life – the effects of acculturation remain in doubt. Indeed, contributors to this volume seem to agree that Jewish Americans have long withstood and even now present subtle yet significant challenges to the melting pot.

In one regard, this year's review is a departure from previous volumes, which juxtaposed previously published material from the scholarly and popular literature. The current edition presents brand new scholarship. What occasioned this change? With the 2002 Association of Jewish Studies conference held in Los Angeles, the Casden Institute found itself at the scholarly center of Jewish studies. The annual AJS conference showcases up-and-coming academic talent alongside the latest work from established leaders in the various fields of Jewish study and provides an opportunity to learn firsthand about the issues of contemporary debate. For this volume, therefore, the institute invited submissions directly from conference participants and affiliates.

The change in format also supports the Casden Institute's

increasing prominence as a scholarly research center. In the past two years, the institute has supported several important research projects conducted by USC faculty and students. For example, the institute provided a dissertation fellowship to USC history candidate Shirli Brautbar, who studies the development of Zionist-related women's organizations in Los Angeles. In addition, a newly created faculty research program supports USC law school professor Nomi Stolzenberg, whose work, featured in this volume, explores custody issues affecting the religious upbringing of children of divorced interfaith families. Another faculty award assists USC Slavic languages professor John Bowlt in his study of Russian-Jewish artists in the United States.

Along with its support for research projects, in the fall of 2003 the institute welcomed its first postdoctoral research associate: sociologist Tobin Belzer, a recent Ph.D. from Brandeis University, who studies the intersection of occupation and identity among young adults working in Jewish professions. Two undergraduate scholarships were also awarded to USC students who have demonstrated leadership in the university's Jewish community.

The Papers

The five scholarly essays in this volume present a rich quilt of Jewish experience across time and between disciplines. In the field of jurisprudence and political philosophy, USC legal historian Nomi Stolzenberg takes a close look at the intellectual underpinnings of the "spiritual custody" cases gaining currency in the American legal system. Focusing on a particularly good and thorough judicial decision, Stolzenberg considers the case of Zummo v. Zummo, in which divorced parents – a practicing Jewish mother and a lapsed-Catholic father – dispute the religious indoctrination of their children. In doing so, they perforce place the children's spiritual identity in the hands of a judge – a state of affairs intrinsically at odds with principles of liberalism and the First Amendment, Stolzenberg contends.

Ted Merwin's reconstruction of shifting themes and preoccupations of New York-based Yiddish theater offers another lens through which the cultural concerns of American Jews come into crisp focus. Concentrating on the theme of materialism and consumerism in the *tsaytbilders* and sweat shop plays exemplified by Osip Dymov's 1919 hit *Bronks Ekspres* and other plays of the era, Merwin, who teaches Judaic studies at Dickinson College, explores the double-edged sword of Jewish integration into the American mainstream and the alienation inherent in the uptown march toward middle class life. His far-reaching study culminates in an overview of contemporary drama, including Tony Kushner's acclaimed *Angels in America*, in which – fulfilling the bitter-sweet promise of full assimilation – the Jewish playwright wrestles not with themes of Jewish particularity but, rather, gay identity.

English scholar Adam Rovner carries the discussion into the realm of comedy, in his historical overview of Jewish humor from Heinrich Heine's *Judenwitz* to Woody Allen's stand-up routines. Rovner contends that so successful has Jewish-American assimilation been that one of its defining traits – the comic pratfalls of its *schlemiels* – has been appropriated by the mass culture to the point that Jewish humor is indistinguishable from American humor in general. To support this theory, Rovner puts Philip Roth's classic *Portnoy's Complaint* under a magnifying glass, with particular attention to the "little man's" Freudian fixation with and anxiety about food and sex.

In the fourth chapter, Michael E. Staub's exploration of the evolving notion of "lessons of the Holocaust" presents a prism through which one can observe the pendulum swings of Jewish-American political thought. Contrary to popular myth, talk of the Holocaust was far from taboo in the postwar years, argues the author, who holds appointments in English and culture studies at Bowling Green State University. References abound in the era's media and public life, as Straub amply documents. By retracing a half-century of American-Jewish rhetoric surrounding the Shoah, Staub turns the defining Jewish tragedy of the modern age into a barometer of shifting domestic politics. The purported "lessons" of the Nazi genocide, he demonstrates, have swung from a moral imperative to fight American racism to a demographic imperative to be fruitful and multiply, with many digressions along the way – and only a recent inkling that lesson-making of any kind might be to trivialize the unspeakable and dishonor the dead.

Lastly, in the area of education, Brandeis University's Meredith Woocher turns the tools of qualitative sociology on the phenomenon of adult Jewish learning, shedding light on why a wave of Jews from all walks of life are returning to *shul* in middle and late life. After spending 100 hours observing and interviewing a group of adult learners at a Melton Mini-Adult School, Woocher reports her findings in the primary spheres of religious activity: believing, belonging and behaving.

In many ways, these topics converge with ongoing activities of the Casden Institute. For example, Staub's political overview dovetails with the institute's Carmen and Louis Warschaw Distinguished Lecture series, exploring the Jewish role in American politics. Now in its sixth year, the series has invited nationally prominent Jewish-American elected officials – such as Sen. Dianne Feinstein, former Rep. Sam Gejdenson, Sen. Joseph Lieberman, Rep. Barney Frank and Sen. Norm Coleman – to weigh in on pressing issues of the day. Staub's Holocaust-themed study as well as Merwin's invocation of the early history of the New York stage serve well to herald the institute's newly endowed Dr. Harold I. Lee Lecture series, which in spring 2003 welcomed classical pianist and author Mona Golabek as its first lecturer/performer. The Grammy-nominated recording artist and radio host wrote *The Children of Willesden Lane*, a memoir of her mother's journey through World War II, made tolerable only through the gift of music. On another cultural note, in October 2002 the Casden Institute co-sponsored, with Yiddishkayt Los Angeles and the Skirball Cultural Center, a program called "New Yiddish Song" exploring contemporary Klezmer music and Yiddish musical traditions through original songs. In a thespian segue that fits together neatly with Merwin's essay on the Yiddish stage, in spring 2003 the Casden Institute collaborated with the L'Chaim Theatre of USC in a production of *The Merchant*, the tale of Shakespeare's Shylock retold in 1932 Berlin.

Meanwhile, Rovner's exploration of the comic *schlemiel* follows well in the wake of the recent collaboration between the

Casden Institute and Writers Bloc in a forum titled "Jewish Comedy Then and Now," featuring comedians Shelley Berman, Schecky Greene, Jeffrey Ross, Jerry Stiller and writer Lawrence Epstein, author of *The Haunted Smile: The Story of Jewish Comedians in America.* Foreshadowing Rovner's careful scholarship, the forum debated how Jewish values, traditions and fears have found voice through comedy and how comedy has historically provided an outlet for tensions between the Jewish and American identity. Other articles in the review, such as Woocher's adult education survey and Stolzenberg's spiritual custody analysis, clearly advance the Casden Institute's overarching goals: to study the evolution of the western Jewish community within American society and to create discourse in the community about the Jewish role in American life.

With this collection of scholarly papers the Casden Institute asks the reader to consider a common theme. Over the past century, the struggle for Jewish acceptance in America seems to have shifted to a struggle *against* Jewish assimilation. Are the boundaries between Jewish life and American society still in flux? What is the family court's proper role in settling disputes over "spiritual custody" of interfaith children? How has the loss of historical perspective on the Holocaust informed modern political values? Why are American Jews turning to the study of religious text late in life? How has the portrayal of Jews in literature, film and theater influenced the blending of Jewish and American cultures? How do we see these questions reflected across disciplines and scholars? Across time and across regions?

While this volume does not propose to address the Jewish role in American life in its entirety, nor to proclaim itself the preeminent authority on the subject, nor even to address every study of importance during the previous year, it does undertake to leave the reader enlightened, intrigued to learn more and in little doubt as to the importance of studying Jewishness and the contributions of Jews to American life.

Chapter One

VALUES:
"Spiritual Custody":
Religious Freedom and
Coercion in the Family

By Nomi Stolzenberg

In our fast-moving modern society, the traditional nuclear family is undone by divorce as often as not. One of divorce's most poignant consequences is the struggle that ensues over the children. A lesser-known, but often jarring, variant of the custody battle is the struggle over the children's religious upbringing. In which tradition should they be raised, if the parents are themselves of different religions, or if one parent is religious and the other is not? Or, in which version of the "same" religion, if parents subscribe to different denominations or personal understandings of the requirements of their faith (e.g., Orthodox versus Reform Judaism, Protestantism versus Catholicism? Baptists versus Methodists? High church versus low?)?

These situations make for contentious and protracted disputes, played out with increasing frequency in our nation's courts. I propose to explore the phenomenon of "spiritual custody," as this concept is evocatively called in the language of American family law, both as a matter of law and political theory. What makes the subject particularly worthy of study is that it lays bare deep and often irreconcilable tensions at the heart of modern liberalism. On one hand, powerful forces of personal choice and autonomy prompt parents to join and exit marital unions at will – and prompt individuals, more generally, to choose their own life path. On the other, parents and society in general put a premium on inculcating moral and cultural values in children – and on fostering religious traditions in and through them. Spiritual custody law is a fascinating site of confrontation between these two impulses.

The tension reflected in the law of spiritual custody between the value of individual autonomy and the desire to preserve religious and cultural traditions is one that pervades the modern world. It has been expressed most vociferously in the battles waged by fundamentalist religious movements against secular and liberal values and political regimes. But fundamentalism is only the most militant, and hardly the most common expression of this tension. Many people who basically identify with modern secular, liberal culture, and hold no truck with religious extremism or violent militancy, nonetheless experience troubling conflicts between the claims of their heritage and the values of liberal, secular society to which they also subscribe.

These tensions are often represented as conflicts that occur between two discrete cultures, each of which is internally unified and singularly opposed to the other. Thus, we commonly understand religious groups that seek to establish their own schools to be involved in an enterprise of protecting "their own" values against the values of the larger society. Spiritual custody cases can likewise be seen as conflicts between religious subgroups and the wider culture. But spiritual custody cases revolve around value-conflicts *within* the family. All too often, discussions of the tension between liberal and religious values rest on the implicit assumption that "the family," figured as the chief vehicle of cultural transmission in society, is an organic unity. Spiritual custody cases remind us of what we all too often lose sight of: that families are beset not only by outside forces but by conflicts internal to the family as well. The very identity of particular family's religious (or nonreligious) creed or culture is internally contested in a spiritual custody case. Recognizing the internally-contested nature of a family's religious/cultural identity creates difficult questions for a liberal polity dedicated to religious tolerance, freedom of belief, and family autonomy. Who has the right to prevail in these cases is uncertain. Indeed, it is unclear that there is any way to resolve these disputes without impinging on *somebody's* autonomy, and offending the basic principles of liberalism. Spiritual custody cases thus bring us into contact with the limits of liberalism, forcing us to reconsider the place of religion both within the family and within the society at large.

The Case of Zummo v. Zummo

In 1988, David and Pamela Zummo, the divorced parents of Adam, Rachel, and Daniel Zummo, appeared before a Pennsylvania family court, seeking resolution of what had become an intractable dispute. Pamela and David disagreed about the religious training of their children. Pamela asked the court to order David to bring the children to their synagogue to attend Sunday school during their weekend visitations with their father. She also asked the court to prohibit David from bringing the children to church with him. David was a "sporadic" Roman Catholic. Pamela was an "actively practicing" Jew. The family court, which heard and ultimately granted, both of Pamela's requests, observed that, "prior to their marriage, mother and father discussed their religious differences and agreed that any children would be raised in the Jewish faith." It further noted that "during the marriage, the Zummo family participated fully in the life of the Jewish faith and community," becoming members of the Norristown Jewish Community Center, attending services and joining a Jewish couples' group at their synagogue, and celebrating the Jewish Sabbath every Friday night until Pamela and David divorced.

Although he never converted, David did not share his religious traditions with his children during the time he was married. A "lapsed" Catholic, he put the faith in which he was raised aside and supported his wife in her aim to give their children a Jewish upbringing. But after their divorce, things changed. David began attending Catholic mass occasionally and wanted to bring his children with him to church and to family functions and holiday celebrations – not regularly, but now and then. He also told Pamela that he did not want to have to take the children to Hebrew school during their weekend visits with him. Testifying in court that "he had no intent to interfere with his children's religious education as Jews or to convert them to Catholicism," David was conciliatory, stating: "I guess I am in agreement with my wife, as far as not creating an identity problem." (Strikingly, David still referred to Pamela as his "wife" after the divorce proceedings.) "It's just that – what my contention is," David falteringly explained to the court, "I don't want to be buried as far as my ability to relate my children and how I relate to my children is really – I mean, what I am is a product of my heritage and my religious training. I don't want to be barred from that." With a little more confidence, he stated his basic legal claim: "What's necessary for me is that I can have the freedom to expose them, maybe not on a regular basis, semi-regular basis, I don't know, but at least have that freedom, respecting her wishes as much as much as possible, and still have the ability to have some way of instilling what's good about my background." Struggling to reconcile this assertion of his religious rights and identity and parental authority with his sense of his "wife's" equal right to the same (and his own earlier commitments), David came to the heart of the matter: his desire as a parent to bond with his children and, more particularly, to bond his children *to* him. Based on his understanding of himself as a "product of my heritage and my religious training," David's desire was, in short, to project his own identity onto his children. Giving voice to the concerns of many "weekend fathers," fearful of estrangement from their children, David plaintively testified, "I am worried about what kind of input I have with my children, and every aspect, timewise," then concluded with a trifle more assertiveness, "I have a lot at stake here, too" (*Zummo* 1160).

What *do* parents have at stake in disputes like these? And how should courts resolve them? These are the basic questions raised by "spiritual custody" cases. Such lawsuits are interesting not only for their inherent human drama – the cases are poignant, often heartbreaking – but also because they bring us face to face with the limits of the constitutional principles that govern them.

Freedom of religion and freedom of choice in matters of belief, more generally, are the fundamental principles of liberalism that govern the legal resolution of spiritual custody disputes, along with such other basic liberal principles as the right not to be controlled or harmed by others and the right not to be controlled or harmed by the state. Courts addressing spiritual custody claims have applied these principles, with more or less consistency, more or less intelligence, and more or less sensitivity, depending on the particular court and the particular judge. In some cases, religious biases appear to have skewed decisions. For example, some judges seem to evince a bias against parents who practice "extreme" unorthodox or non-mainstream faiths, such as Jehovah's Witnesses who include their children in their proselytizing efforts, or Christian Scientists who deny their children medical treatment. Other judges to seem to exhibit a more general bias against religion, in favor of the "modern," secular parent. Still more prefer generic "religiosity" over parents who profess and practice no religious faith. More often than not, however, judges seem to bend over backward to avoid these sorts of results, striving to attain a position of judicial "impartiality" and "neutrality" vis-à-vis different religious faiths and vis-à-vis the choice between religious and non-religious parents (Schneider). This, the legal community generally agrees, is required by the basic principles of freedom of religion and conscience, and the prohibition against state "establishments" or "entanglements" with religion, enshrined in the First Amendment (Schneider, Beschle, 416, Compton v. Gilmore).

But no matter how much they strain to eliminate bias from their judgments, no matter how conscientiously they apply the basic constitutional principles of liberty, equality, neutrality, and tolerance that govern our legal system, judges inevitably end up

violating these principles in spiritual custody cases. Even when
they decline to intervene – when they effectively decide *not* to
decide, in other words – they find that they have in effect sided
with one of the parents against the other, despite themselves and
their best intentions. For a decision not to adjudicate a spiritual
custody dispute in effect supports the parent who opposes the
action.

This is exactly what happened in the *Zummo v. Zummo* case,
on appeal. David challenged the family court's decision ordering
him to arrange for the children's attendance at Hebrew school
during their weekend visits with him and prohibiting him from
taking the children "to religious services contrary to the Jewish
faith." Though the family court had made allowances for bringing
the children to Catholic family events, including Christmas, Easter,
weddings, and funerals, its basic decision had been to place the
children in the spiritual as well as physical, custody of the mother.
Adopting the arguments made by Pamela's lawyer, the family court
judge had taken the view that exposure to both religions might
"unfairly confuse and disorient" them, and that "it was in the
children's best interests to preserve the stability of their religious
beliefs." The court of appeals overturned the trial court's decision
and rejected all of the arguments put forth on its behalf.
Emphasizing "the constitutional prerequisite of 'benign neutrality'
towards both parent's religious viewpoints," the appellate court
forswore the authority to favor one of the parent's right to spiritual
custody over the other. But in doing so, the court effectively
sided with the father's contention that "children would benefit
from a bi-cultural upbringing and should therefore be exposed to
the religion of each parent" (*Zummo* 1141).

It is of course a characteristically liberal idea that we can avoid
taking sides by simply exposing people to competing viewpoints,
and declining to favor any particular one. But this liberal policy
of non-exclusion through exposure is itself a particular contested
position. To refuse to favor one parent's claim to spiritual custody
over another is not so much to avoid adjudicating the conflict as
it is to favor the liberal position in that conflict. Liberalism is
itself one of the antagonistic points of view in the contest between

competing viewpoints about how children should be brought up
– which is to say that, paradoxically, liberalism is antagonistic to
itself.

The inherent contradictions of liberalism, and the impossibility
of escaping them, are made painfully clear in spiritual custody
cases like *Zummo v. Zummo*. *Zummo* is a particularly good case
to drive the point home because the judicial opinion that it
generated on appeal avoided the mistakes often made in spiritual
custody adjudications, yet still failed to avoid contradicting the
very liberal premises upon which it rests. Authored by Judge
John Kelly, of the Pennsylvania Superior Court, the *Zummo v.
Zummo* opinion is unusually sensitive to the various interests and
needs at stake in the case, as well as to the various parties' different
points of view. It is exceptionally thorough in its canvassing of
the various theoretical and doctrinal frameworks that could be
used to resolve spiritual custody controversies. And it offers an
astute and at times profound analysis of the shortcomings of each
of the available approaches. Judge Kelly's opinion is, in a word,
wise, a term not often affixed to judicial opinions these days.
Nonetheless, it was no more successful in resolving the dispute
in a manner consistent with the liberal principles of religious
tolerance, freedom, and neutrality than other court decisions.

The fact that Judge Kelly's failure cannot be dismissed as the
result of intellectual or moral shortcomings on his part requires
us to consider the possibility that the failure reflects limitations
built into liberalism itself. Judge Kelly scrupulously avoided the
various lapses of judgment that have marred judicial decisions
handed down in other spiritual cases. Nonetheless, his opinion
betrayed some of the basic constitutional principles of liberalism
that guided him. It thus reveals the inherent contradictions of
liberalism. At the same time, it raises again the question of what
exactly is at stake in spiritual custody disputes. What did David
gain, and what did Pamela lose? And what did the children stand
to gain or lose?

The Problem of Religious Freedom
and Control in a Liberal Society

In many cases where parents have religious differences, they manage to work them out, or at least live with them, without destroying each other and without resorting to the law. But in a growing number of cases, protracted religious disputes have led parents to petition judges to grant one of them more or less exclusive control over their children's religious upbringing, just as Pamela Zummo did. *Zummo v. Zummo* provides a lens through which we can better understand what parents are trying to gain out of winning such a right of control, as well as what is potentially lost – and what might (and should) lie beyond anyone's control. Indeed, *Zummo v. Zummo* confronts us with the limits of control, with the limits of both parental and legal control over "spiritual development." Before turning to the *Zummo* opinion, however, it may be helpful to elaborate the basic philosophical dilemma expressed in spiritual custody cases – the dilemma of freedom and control – in non-legal terms.

It is a truism about modern, liberal societies that they make religious affiliations voluntary – and therefore vulnerable. Religious and social critics of liberalism have long charged that faith is rendered vulnerable in liberal societies precisely as a result of its being made voluntary (Stolzenberg & Myers, 648, Bentwich, 147-72).

The threat posed by liberalism to religious faith is downplayed in the mainstream political culture through a variety of rhetorical devices, for example, by emphasizing the freedom *to* affiliate with a religion of one's choice. (Recall how Senator Joseph Lieberman won the crowds over during his run for vice-President with his statement that the First Amendment stands for freedom *of* religion, not *from* religion.) (Lieberman). The reality, of course, is that freedom of religion *entails* freedom from religion. Consequently, as the critics have long claimed, liberalism has always posed a threat to religious groups.

But, what kind of threat? There has always been something mystifying about liberalism's adversarial relationship with religious groups and traditions. For one thing, it is undeniably true that liberalism mandates religious tolerance and protects the right to participate in religious associations. Critics of liberal tolerance have argued that these core values produce a culture of individualism that, paradoxically, undermines religious groups and their traditions. Historical experience largely supports their claim that Enlightenment ideals of emancipation and individual rights undercut the traditional forms of communal autonomy and authority that historically undergirded religious groups, as well as their further claim that the values of diversity and freedom of conscience led many people to abandon traditional faith. Yet religious groups have simply not "withered away." On the contrary, Americans are routinely – and accurately – described as a highly religious people (Carter).

If the hallmark of liberal society is the individual's freedom to decide which religion to belong to, or whether to belong to any religion at all, the great tendency of individuals in American society has been to embrace religious affiliation. Although, as a logical matter, the freedom of religion implies the freedom not to practice any, as a sociological matter, the majority of Americans have exercised their right to religious freedom in conformity with Lieberman's slogan: "freedom *of* religion," not "freedom *from.*" Like marriage (another area of social relations where liberals fought hard to establish the "freedom not to"), religion seems to be one of those social institutions most Americans can't get enough of. Given the choice, rather than avoid these institutions, Americans continue to enter both marriage and religion with undiminished hopes and expectations. Even when their marital or religious affiliations dissolve, their strong tendency is to attach themselves to yet another marital partner or religious tradition, rather than abandon marriage or religion altogether. (If, as has often been observed, Americans have a penchant for "serial monogamy," we might justly observe that they have a similar predilection for "serial faith.")

Notwithstanding how indulgent Americans are of romantic and religious changes of heart, the common practices of serial monogamy and serial faith both demonstrate an abiding cultural preference for affiliation over un-affiliation, for "freedom of" over "freedom from." (Consider our attitudes toward our politicians: one who takes a new wife is eminently forgivable, one who adopts a new faith is positively exemplary; but the politician who espouses no spouse or creed is going to have a hard time getting elected.) Of course there are Americans who opt out of marriage and religion altogether – but surprisingly few given their supposedly optional character.

The American penchant for religious affiliation could be interpreted as showing that the critics' view that liberalism makes religion voluntary and therefore vulnerable is only half-true. Perhaps the truth is that religion has become a voluntary affair, but being voluntary has not made religion vulnerable to disaffection in the way that the critics predicted. This position has some intuitive plausibility. But are our religious affiliations really voluntary? This is supposedly what distinguishes a liberal from a traditional society, according to both liberalism's critics and its defenders (Stolzenberg & Myers, Richards, 105-21). But perhaps this common understanding is wrong. The critics of liberalism may have it wrong on both scores – maybe the truth is that religion in a liberal society like America is neither voluntary nor vulnerable, or at least not *as* voluntary or *as* vulnerable as the critics have argued. And perhaps the surprising durability of religion in America does not so much reflect American "preferences" or "choice" as it demonstrates the very same kind of social mechanisms that ensured the perpetuation of religious cultures in traditional, non-liberal societies.

Liberal political theory pictures competing religious and cultural belief-systems as constituting a sort of "marketplace of ideas," and it pictures people as consumers who get to make selections from this cultural-religious-philosophical marketplace much the same way we select material goods from the marketplace – without the rigid constraints on identity that prevailed in traditional societies. But examining what *leads* people to make the "choices" about religion that they do never reveals individuals, unconstrained by prior beliefs and cultural attachments, simply making a rational, detached choice about what to believe and where to belong. The "isolated selves" of liberal mythology, "cut loose from all social ties" and freely choosing their beliefs and attachments from a menu of available options, are just that, a myth – at best, a useful theoretical construct; at worst, a distortion of reality (Walzer 9-10) We do not emerge from the chrysalis of childhood as the "unencumbered" individuals pictured in liberal political theory (Walzer 10, Sandel 538). Our childhood experiences shape and constrain us and, to a great extent, determine who we are. We bear the imprint of our earliest cultural experiences even when we struggle to shake them off.

All this we know. What we do not know is how to square this familiar knowledge of ourselves as creatures of the cultures into which we are born with the equally familiar picture of ourselves as autonomous individuals exercising freedom of choice.

The standard way of reconciling the contradiction is to invoke a certain conception of "the family." Liberal political theory typically conceives of the family as an "intermediate institution" (Dailey, 1836) that constitutes a social space that hovers in between self and society, individual and group. As such, the family is supposed to resolve the tension between the cultural conditioning that necessarily shapes us as we grow and the state of freedom and autonomy that supposedly awaits us when we are grown. Although the family is a private collection of individuals from the point of view of the state, from the standpoint of the individual, the family is a group that shapes and constrains the individuals within it. The family thus combines qualities of the individual and the group and, somehow, "mediates" between our qualities of individuality and groupness. In the same vein, the family is also thought to somehow "mediate" between the forces of acculturation and social conditioning to which we all are subject and the values of liberty and choice that we are supposed to possess. Thus, the family is pictured as carrying out different social functions that stand in tension with each other. On the one hand, liberal theory entrusts the family with the "communitarian" function of transmitting the traditions of a particular culture from one generation to the next. It likewise sees the family as serving the "cultural pluralist" function of ensuring the ongoing existence of diverse sub-cultures, rather than having a single homogenous

culture society-wide. On the other hand, the family is expected
to fulfill the classically "liberal" function of ensuring that children
develop the ability to exercise the "normal" faculties of reason
and choice. Looking at these various social tasks entrusted to the
family through the lens of the market metaphors which structure
liberal thought, one might say that the family serves to foster
both the supply and the demand functions of the "marketplace of
ideas." On the supply side, families, by virtue of their
communitarian and cultural pluralist functions, serve as the
vehicles through which the different religious and ethnic sub-
cultures that make up a pluralistic society are transmitted and
delivered to the cultural marketplace. On the demand side, the
family's liberal function is to produce the autonomous individuals,
the informed consumers, who are capable of choosing from that
marketplace. Through appropriate child-rearing, the idea is that
families gradually nurture the capacity to think and make choice,
allowing the autonomous individual to emerge. And thus the
contradiction between our cultural dependence and our right to
individual independence is magically resolved (Dailey 1826-
1850).

The problem remains, however, that these functions stand in
tension with each other. Besides invoking magical terms like
"intermediate," and "mediate," liberal political thought never
really explains how the tensions are resolved. If a family succeeds
in transmitting a particular faith or cultural identity, then it follows
that individuals raised in that family are, to say the least,
predisposed to "choose" that faith/identity from the menu of
available cultural and religious options. This is indeed a rather
understated way of making the point. (Other commentators speak
of "value-inculcation" or – the scare word – "indoctrination.")
But whatever terms are used to describe the concern, the point is
the operation of powerful forces of socialization or acculturation,
which call into question how much of a choice we really have in
determining our religious or cultural identity as adults.

The standard way of "solving" the problem of predisposition
or indoctrination is to say that families are (or should be)
sufficiently open and supportive of the development of the normal

capacity of reason that children grow up to be able to make choices for themselves. In other words, the upbringing provided by a family must be sufficiently, though minimally, liberal. A sufficiently liberal upbringing means simply that children are not completely insulated from exposure to alternative ways of life, nor completely "indoctrinated," i.e., deprived of the ability to think for themselves. With the emphasis here on "completely," liberal theorists of children's education generally agree that these requirements are not inconsistent with allowing parents broad latitude in controlling the upbringing of their children and limiting their religious and cultural horizons. So long as the normal faculties of reasoning and independent judgment are allowed to develop, and so long as an "adequate" range of choices is presented to children once they are grown, liberal political theory generally holds that letting parents place limits on their children's cultural horizons is not only permissible but necessary to social development (Gutmann 43-47, Macedo 237-38).

This conception of the family providing a liberal education or upbringing depends on several questionable assumptions. The "communitarian" function is granted wide berth on the theory that allowing the family to inculcate the values of a particular religion or culture in children does not preclude (and in fact may be a prerequisite to) the emergence of the child's faculties of independent reason and choice. But the compatibility of the liberal and communitarian functions – the possibility of a choice-promoting education existing alongside a family's inculcation of particular values; the possibility of individual independence coexisting with cultural dependency within a single individual – is merely asserted, never explained. Rather than demystifying the way the "mediating" function of the family works, this line of argument simply repeats the familiar mystifications. How the control that our parents exercise over the shape of our identity ever ends – how it is, for example, that someone raised in an Amish family, or in a Hasidic family, ends up leaving the community in which she was raised – are questions that never really get answered in most treatments of the family by liberal political theorists. It is left more or less a mystery how the cultural forces that exercise such a powerful effect over the formation of our identities when we are young cease to constrain us when we become adults – or how, if they do continue to shape our identities, our choices and judgments can really be said to be "free."

If the family's communitarian function of cultural transmission creates one set of problems, its liberal function of cultivating reason and choice creates more. Cultural conditioning, according to the liberal theory of the family, does not prevent the emergence of the autonomous adult, capable of choosing for herself from the marketplace of ideas — so long as certain, fairly minimal, conditions are met. So long, that is, as the family refrains from total indoctrination, and so long as it does not completely shut out awareness of alternative ways of life, the family is understood to produce individuals who are as capable of rejecting their upbringing as embracing it, depending solely on their own personal inclinations. In other words, a liberal upbringing is supposed to permit (though not require) people to transcend, or escape, their family's religious heritage and upbringing. But, as the *Zummo* case suggests, even a liberal approach to upbringing tends to reproduce itself. (Just as Jewish families tend to produce Jews, and Catholic families tend to produce Catholics, liberal families tend to produce liberals.) Of course, we are only speaking of tendencies, not strict determinism. (People raised in liberal families sometimes rebel against their parents' liberalism, just as sometimes people raised in Jewish families sometimes reject their parents' faith.) But the fact that people sometimes reject, and almost always modify, their parents' faith does not contradict the formative impact of our upbringings on our identity. Thus, the problem of cultural predisposition or "indoctrination" – the problem of reconciling parental control over upbringing with the value of freedom of choice – remains.

Perhaps the gravest challenge to the usual way of attempting to reconcile parental authority and cultural conditioning with free choice stems from yet another weakness in the liberal model of the family: an unspoken assumption that "the family" is internally homogeneous and bears a single identity. The assumption of the culturally homogenous, unitary family clearly underlies the usual communitarian and cultural-pluralist constructions of the family as a vehicle of cultural transmission. In all of these accounts, the family is routinely construed as a unitary entity, as if religious and cultural differences within a family do not occur. Liberal theory may voice an occasional hesitation over parental control tending to suppress the emergence of differences between parents and children, but the point, then, is that such differences *are suppressed*. Differences between parents are usually not even mentioned. The tacit assumption is that parents share a common religious (or secular) identity, which they jointly inculcate in their children.

Obviously, this assumption of parental unity is highly unrealistic. Parents often differ in their religious beliefs and practices, some finding their way to compromise, others collapsing into conflict. But if the family harbors religious conflicts, then our understanding of the tension between freedom of choice and parental control has to be significantly revised. The problem can no longer be seen simply in terms of one party (the parents) impinging on the freedom of choice of another (the child). Nor can the solution depend on an understanding of the family – or even of the individual – as embodying a single, homogeneous culture or identity. Instead, we need to develop a picture of how multiple parties vie for parental authority and the right to exercise control over the "spiritual development" of their children – and over each other.

Spiritual custody cases shine a spotlight on the complex dynamics of compulsion versus freedom in the family. It is tempting to view these cases – still few but growing in number – as anomalous, as if they only represented "dysfunctional" families, and there were other, "functional" families that still answered to the old assumptions of religious unity and satisfactorily resolved the tension between our dependency on cultural conditioning and the value of individual autonomy and freedom of choice. But just as medicine and psychology have historically used the study of pathology as a window into physical and mental health, so too the study of spiritual custody cases reveals dynamics common to all families in a world governed by the principles of religious liberty, family autonomy, and freedom of choice.

Spiritual custody suits exhibit the family *in extremis*: conflicted, in pain, bound by fierce attachments, and pulled apart by competing loyalties – in other words, the typical family in an exaggerated form. Far from being anomalous, spiritual custody cases throw into relief the struggles for control and personal freedom that occur between parents, and between parents and children, in families both "broken" and "intact," interfaith and intra-faith, religious and secular, traditional and modern. Most of these spiritual custody disputes simply never make it to court. Why some families' religious disputes erupt into legal proceedings, while most never do, is best explained by examining the legal doctrines that govern such disputes.

The Law of Spiritual Custody

Spiritual custody cases are a relatively new legal phenomenon. The first publicly recorded litigation of a spiritual claim appears to have occurred in 1867 (*Cole v. Cole*). Litigation over spiritual custody remained quite rare until the 1950's. Today, there are hundreds, perhaps thousands, of recorded spiritual custody cases.

The dramatic rise in the number of spiritual custody cases is generally attributed to the confluence of several fundamental changes in family-related social and legal practices. Perhaps the most common explanation refers to the increase in the number of interfaith marriages. The assumption underlying this explanation is that people who marry from different religious backgrounds are more likely to fall into disputes over the religious upbringing of their children. Even when parents enter marriage having reached some kind of agreement, as when a spouse converts, or one simply agrees to defer to the other's religious preferences, the chance of such an agreement breaking down haunts the intermarriage scenario, as borne out in cases like *Zummo v. Zummo*.

Divorce is another factor commonly cited as a cause of the rise in spiritual custody cases. All spiritual custody claims are made in the context of the custody proceedings that follow divorce (or its functional equivalent, the separation of unmarried partners).

This is so because courts are generally barred from adjudicating disputes between parents who are married to each other under the legal doctrine of "family privacy." This doctrine denies courts the authority to intervene in family disputes, save for extreme situations when children are clearly at risk of being seriously harmed by their parents (as in cases of child endangerment or abuse and neglect). But it only applies when parents are married to each other; once a legal separation or divorce occurs, courts not only may but must intervene in parental disputes (Gregory 165-67).

With around 50% of marriages now ending in divorce, it stands to reason that there would be a rise in litigation over family affairs, including disputes over spiritual custody. Yet another factor cited as a cause of the rise in the number of spiritual custody claims is the change in the legal standard used to adjudicate child custody. Until the early nineteenth century, when divorce was still rare, the law gave fathers exclusive custody of their children as a general rule under the doctrine of *patria potestas*. This was of a piece with the prevailing view of the father as the head of the family, exercising rightful authority not just over his children but also over his wife (Black and Cantor 4-10).

So long as fathers held exclusive authority over their children as a matter of law, legal disputes between parents over their children's upbringing simply could not occur. Perhaps surprisingly, this bar on judicial intervention in family disputes held fast even after the doctrine of *patria potestas* was abandoned. In the early 19th century, courts began to reject the traditional paternal preference, embracing in its stead a legal preference in favor of placing children in the custody of their mothers, codified in the doctrine of the "tender years presumption." But though this shift from a paternal to a maternal preference seemed to represent a rejection of the old patriarchal custody regime, it perpetuated the basic patriarchal assumption that the family is a unit presided over by a single custodial authority or head of household. Just as the traditional doctrine of paternal authority had denied mothers the right to challenge fathers' decisions about their children's upbringing, the maternal preference, which awarded child custody to the mother, effectively precluded fathers from interfering with most of the decisions that custodial mothers made. The mother, in effect, became the father, for all practical purposes. That is, she became the head of the household and the sole custodian, in most cases, both physical and "spiritual."

By effectively eliminating one of the parents from the legal picture, and denying, first her, then him, the opportunity to claim a legal right to "spiritual custody," both the paternal preference and the subsequently favored maternal preference served to create the illusion – and, to a significant extent, the reality – of a family united under the authority of a single custodian (Fineman 733-34). All this changed with feminism and the advent of new standards that purported to give mothers and fathers equal rights. The presumption in favor of awarding custody to the mother was displaced by a new child custody doctrine that rejected both paternal and maternal preferences in favor of case-by-case inquiries into what would serve the best interests of a particular child.

In theory, either parent is eligible to receive custody under this version of the best interests standard. In practice, however, mothers continued to receive custody of their children in much the same rate as under the tender years presumption when the best-interests regime was first adopted, both because fathers rarely sought custody, and because courts continued to believe that it was in children's best interest to be raised by their mothers. To this day, mothers are much more likely to become the sole custodians of their children than fathers are in cases of divorce. But there has been a significant move in the direction of shared custody between fathers and mothers resulting from the confluence of the feminist movement's call for gender-neutrality in the area of child custody and an emerging father's rights movement, asserting the rights of fathers to custody, control and participation in their children's upbringing. Together these two movements have given rise to a preference for joint custody, and other forms of shared parenting. Though fathers actually seeking custody remain a minority, a clear trend has nonetheless emerged favoring joint custody as a norm (Kandel 145-148).

Thus, the path has been cleared for parents, each now endowed with legally-recognized rights of authority over their children, to enter into spiritual custody disputes. Unlike the earlier regimes of child custody law, which effectively suppressed such disputes by lodging parental authority in a single "head," the combination of the best interests of the child standard and the legal preference for joint custody has opened the door for parents to disagree and to bring their disagreements into the courtroom.

It is not at all surprising that commentators should have identified intermarriage, feminism, divorce, and the various new legal doctrines, such as the best interests of the child standard and the joint custody preference, as "causes" of spiritual custody disputes. But this is just to say that in the past the law actively suppressed the emergence of spiritual custody disputes. What feminism and the new child custody standards have served to do is not so much *cause* spiritual custody disputes as *remove* the legal obstacles that prevented these disputes from being expressed and adjudicated in the public forum of law.

Disagreements between parents in private were never so rare as the public record of litigated disputes would suggest, even before the advent of feminism, gender-neutral custody standards, and the widespread occurrence of divorce. Nor were such disputes limited to cases of interfaith marriages. The notion that women and men had different approaches to the religious training of their children was a commonplace Victorian thought, and what the Victorians had in mind was surely not a man and a woman coming from different religious traditions. Rather, they subscribed to a general belief that women were more scrupulous in their moral and religious observance, and more effective at inculcating values in children of tender years. (It was of course precisely this idea that gave rise to the tender years presumption). The Victorians did not need the stimulus of feminism, intermarriage, or divorce to perceive the possibility of conflicts occurring between mothers and fathers over their children's spiritual development, which strongly suggests that the root causes of spiritual custody disputes lie deeper than the supposed dysfunctions of contemporary life.

To seek the causes of spiritual custody disputes is to return to the question of what is at stake in spiritual custody disputes. What motivates them? Or, to put it more precisely, what motivates the parents who ask for spiritual custody, and what motivates the parents who resist them? The factors adduced in conventional explanations, divorce, intermarriage, and the advent of legal standards granting mothers and fathers equal rights, merely created an opening for parents to stage legal disputes over their children's upbringing. What rushes in to fill that opening is something infinitely more complex than the conventional explanations suggest. Those complexities are nowhere better illustrated, and analyzed, than in the appellate court opinion handed down in the case of *Zummo v. Zummo*. It is to that case that we now return.

Zummo v. Zummo Redux

Zummo v. Zummo framed its analysis in terms of the competing interests that parents have in religious freedom and parental control. But rather than presenting a simple contest between one parent with an interest in religious freedom and one parent with an interest in parental control, the *Zummo* opinion offered a complex picture of mixed motives on the part of each parent.

A less subtle analysis might have portrayed Pamela as the parent desirous of establishing religious control and David as the champion of religious freedom. This would be a fairly standard liberal take on the case. Liberalism, after all, depends on such dichotomies as freedom versus control, choice versus compulsion, and neutrality versus indoctrination. Exposing people to a range of diverse ideas, without making value-judgments about which is better, is thought to be a very different thing from inculcating people with the values of a particular belief-system, the ostensible difference being that only the former leaves people to free "make up their own minds."

Pamela asked the court for the authority to inculcate her religious beliefs in her children; David asked for the freedom to expose the children to "what's good about my background," while "respecting [Pamela's] wishes as much as possible." Pamela argued that exposure to the conflicting religious traditions of

Catholicism and Judaism would cause the children suffering and harm – emotional suffering, in the form of stress and confusion, and the further harm consisting of the destabilization of their established beliefs. David contended that "the children would benefit from a bi-cultural upbringing and should therefore be exposed to the religion of each parent" (*Zummo* 1142). These differences are readily translated into the standard dichotomies of liberal thought, with Pamela being seen as the upholder of the traditional values of value-inculcation, parental control, and authority, and David standing on the opposite side of the dichotomy, defending the liberal values of neutral exposure, diversity, and freedom of choice.

But to frame the contest between David and Pamela in this way would be to miss the point that the tension between the desire for control (over one's children, one's former spouse, and one's self) and the desire for freedom is a struggle that takes place within the breast of each parent, as well as between the two. Notwithstanding the real differences between what Pamela and David wanted for their children (and for themselves), the opinion in *Zummo v. Zummo* revealed that both parents had an equal interest safeguarding their religious freedom *and* in establishing their parental control and authority. What made the case hard was not that one parent wanted these rights and the other did not. The problem, as Judge Kelly notes, was rather that, as a matter of law, "both parents have rights to inculcate religious beliefs in their children," now that we have abandoned the old "gender stereotypes" that used to endow one parent with the exclusive authority of the head of the household (*Zummo* 1135, 1157).

In a spiritual custody dispute, both parents seek control and authority, even when one parent is seeking the authority to instill the values of a secular, liberal, multi-cultural upbringing. This recognition undermines the core idea of liberalism that control and freedom are separable and dichotomous. Judge Kelly drew this recognition out of a careful analysis of the various proposed ways of resolving spiritual custody cases.

Lawyers, judges, and legal commentators have so far come up with three basic ways of handling spiritual custody disputes:

One is a general posture of non-intervention in spiritual custody disputes, favored by many judges. This approach is based on the belief that judges cannot adjudicate spiritual custody disputes without offending the constitutional principles of freedom of religion and the separation of church and state.

The second leading approach, also adopted in many spiritual custody cases, allows judges a broad license to decide if restricting the behavior of one of the parents, and conferring the exclusive rights of spiritual custody on the other, would be in a child's best interests. This approach involves the application of the best-interests standard that has generally governed child custody proceedings since the demise of the traditional presumptions in favor of fathers and mothers, respectively. It basically involves making an open-ended inquiry into the impact of each of the parent's religious practices (or non-religious) on the child or children involved, with an eye towards protecting them from parental practices that will cause them "harm." The defining characteristic of this approach – indeed, the only thing that distinguishes it from the general principle against judicial intervention – is that it accepts a broad definition of harm. Courts following this approach seek to protect children from potential, as opposed to actual, harms, including psychological "harms," such as stress and confusion, which are commonly alleged to result from exposing children to conflicting religious traditions. Such an expansive conception of harm provides an ever-ready justification for intervening in spiritual custody disputes.

The non-interventionist approach, by contrast, resists defining harm to children in such expansive terms. It is not that the non-interventionist approach eschews the best-interests standard, which courts today unanimously agree should govern all child custody proceedings. It is rather that it relies on a different understanding of what the best interest of a child *is*. Advocates of the non-interventionist approach agree that judges should intervene in cases where a child is threatened with serious harm – for example, in cases when a parent's religious convictions require him to withhold medical treatment, or prompt her to teach the child that the other parent is condemned to eternal damnation and must be shunned. The difference between this approach and the more discretionary application of the best-interests standard lies in the narrower conception of harms justifying judicial intervention. For practical purposes, this makes all the difference in the world. More precisely, it marks the difference between a general rule of non-intervention in spiritual disputes (subject only to a narrow exception for cases where children are seriously endangered), and the opposite legal regime, a general rule of subjecting spiritual custody disputes to judicial adjudication (with spiritual custody awards granted routinely as a matter of judicial discretion).

Yet a third approach has been proposed for resolving spiritual custody disputes, which seeks to navigate between the constitutional concerns that militate against judicial intervention and the concern over children's welfare that underlies the more expansive best-interests approach. The proponents of this approach have mostly been scholars (courts have resisted it), though a number of lawyers, including Pamela Zummo's lawyer, have argued for its adoption on behalf of clients seeking to establish spiritual custody. This third approach encourages parents to enter into agreements, or contracts, stipulating the religious upbringing of their children, and calls upon courts to enforce these private agreements when and if one of the parents reneges on his or her earlier commitments.

After surveying all three of these leading legal theories, the non-interventionist principle, the discretionary best-interests approach, and the contractualist approach, Judge Kelly adopted the first, observing that "judges and state officials are deemed ill-equipped to second-guess parents, and are precluded from intervening" in parental disputes, save for emergency situations where the behavior of one of the parents is actually endangering the child, as in cases of child abuse and neglect. Judge Kelly rested this conclusion partly on general principles of constitutional law that seemed to be vindicated by the non-interventionist approach, and partly on the absence of better alternatives, given the weaknesses he perceived in the other two approaches.

The case that Judge Kelly makes against the best-interests

and contractualist theories is indeed compelling. Unfortunately, the case he makes against them applies equally well to the approach he leaves standing, the position disfavoring judicial intervention. In the end, Judge Kelly was forced to intervene and make a decision, even though his decision was only not to decide. But that, as I suggested above, is as value-laden and as meddlesome a decision as any other, paradoxical as that may be. For the decision not to intervene allowed David to carry out the "bi-cultural upbringing" that he favored against Pamela's wishes.

How alert Judge Kelly was to this paradox of non-intervention is uncertain. That he was generally alert to the paradoxes of liberalism vis-à-vis religious disputes is evident from his treatment of the other two leading theories of how to resolve spiritual custody disputes.

Perhaps the most innovative aspect of Judge Kelly's opinion lies in his treatment of the contractualist theory. A number of commentators and a few judges have argued that the best way to deal with religious differences over children's upbringing is through the mechanism of private contract (Freeman 89-91, Strauber 1008-10). As a policy matter, contractualists suggest that spouses should discuss their differences and hammer out agreements about the religious identity and upbringing of their children. Ideally, such agreements would take the form of a written contract that could readily be consulted in the event of a disagreement. But some agreements might be more informal: an oral agreement or even an implicit understanding between parents concerning their children's religious identity. According to contractualist logic, such agreements are best entered into before the children are born, or even before the couple marry. But they might also be formed at a later point in time. Either way, the theory is that it is better for parents to settle their differences themselves than to descend into bitter conflict and have a court impose a decision on them.

In addition to preventing courts from inappropriately intervening in religious controversies and infringing on parental autonomy, a private agreement is supposed to have the salutary effect of getting parents to resolve their differences in advance, before real conflicts arise, so that either they never arise, or, if they do, it is clear how to resolve them. The appeal of contracting as a strategy for avoiding or managing religious conflicts has led many rabbis, ministers, and priests to institute the contemporary practice of pre-marital counseling, focused in good part on getting the partners to think about these issues and work out more or less formalized pre-nuptial agreements regarding the children's upbringing. (Such pre-marital services also supposedly serve the gate-keeping function of encouraging people whose religious differences seem unbridgeable to reconsider their plans). Formal statements of one party's commitment to raise the children in particular faith are also a typical part of the religious conversion process in some religions.

Proponents of the contractualist approach argue that courts hearing spiritual custody cases should look for evidence of such commitments or contracts and enforce them when they are to be found. They strenuously oppose the idea that spiritual custody contracts should not be enforced when a parent has had a change of heart. This is precisely what contracts are for, they argue: not only to ensure that the people to whom we make commitments get what they bargained for, but also to allow us to bind ourselves. In other words, when one makes a spiritual custody contract, it is a commitment not just to one's partner, but to oneself. It is binding the present self against the possible future self – the person one might evolve into in the future – who might subvert one's present wishes. If one couldn't bind oneself, couldn't promise now to refuse to indulge potential changes of heart in the future, then how, the contractualist asks, could one make commitments at all?

The contractualist argument says: if a person chooses to bind herself, as an expression of her own free will, why not let her? Isn't such a course consistent with the fundamental liberal value of freedom of choice? We accept this logic all the time in common contracting situations with commercial actors. Why not apply the same logic here? What is different about contracts for the exchange of spiritual custody rights, as opposed to material goods?

Two obvious differences come to mind, though whether those differences argue in favor of or against the enforcement of spiritual custody contracts remains to be seen. One key difference is that the subject of a spiritual custody dispute is not a material commodity but is rather a matter of religious identity and faith. The other key difference, of course, is that besides the two parties who enter into an agreement (the two parents), there's a third party directly affected by the agreement, though not a party to it: the child.

As one court put it, punning on the contract law doctrine of third-party beneficiaries, the child is a "third party maleficiary" to the contract (*Hackett* 482). This formulation reminds us that the most vulnerable people in spiritual custody conflicts are the children. The question, though, is what harms them. Are children harmed by the breakdown of spiritual custody agreements and the refusal of courts to abide by them, leaving them at the mercy of warring parents and caught in the middle of antagonistic cultures? Or are they actually more subject to harm when spiritual custody contracts are enforced? Proponents of the contractualist approach appeal to the liberal values of freedom of choice and freedom of contract. But they clinch their argument with the notion that conflicting approaches to religious upbringing cause children harm. The whole point of spiritual custody agreements is that they are supposed to spare children the sufferings thought to result from being subjected to contrary child-rearing approaches. From this point of view, children are the intended beneficiaries of spiritual custody contracts, not their "maleficiaries." They only stand to become "maleficiaries" in the case when courts refuse to enforce them.

This idea resonates with widely held contemporary views about children's psychological needs and interests. Conventional wisdom dictates that stability and consistency serve children's best interests, and, conversely, that change and conflict produce emotional stress and psychological harm. More specifically, exposing children to conflicting religious views and different styles of upbringing is widely believed (as Pamela Zummo argued) to cause them stress and confusion. In short, pain and suffering result from having more than one "spiritual custodian" with conflicting practices and beliefs. By this account, parents should be encouraged to form spiritual custody contracts, and they should be required by law to carry them out, precisely because such contracts protect the interests of children. In other words, spiritual custody contracts are to be enforced for the sake of the children.

The case for spiritual custody contracts thus depends on the principle of promoting the best interests of the children. It depends, however, on a particular view about what the best interests of the children are. The understanding of children on which the contractualist argument rests equates their interests with stability and consistency, and, conversely, holds that children are harmed by instability, inconsistency, and conflict in their upbringing. At first glance, this may seem utterly unexceptionable, the statement of an uncontroversial truth rather than a particular, contestable point of view. Indeed, popularized by contemporary psychology, this view has largely succeeded in reshaping the practice of child custody law; it would be hard to find dissenters. But in the context of spiritual custody disputes, it functions in essence as an updated version of the old principle of family unity, decked out in the modern therapeutic language. After all, instability, inconsistency, and conflict can only be avoided by ensuring that there is only one spiritual authority – either a head of the household or the mythical, magically-unified, family. A consistent, stable approach to a child's upbringing can be achieved, and conflict avoided, only if there is in fact a unified parental team, as when both parents make and remain committed to an agreement about how to raise their children; or, in the event of a breakdown in the agreement, if one of the parents alone is granted exclusive rights of spiritual authority.

The arguments that Pamela made in *Zummo v. Zummo* show clearly how the contractualist argument in favor of enforcing spiritual custody agreements depends on this underlying view of children's needs. Not only did she argue that exposure to David's Catholic practices would cause the children painful stress and confusion, but she also simultaneously asserted the existence of a spiritual custody agreement. Although no formal written ante-nuptial contract had been executed, it was undisputed that "the Zummo's had orally agreed prior to their marriage that any children to their marriage would be raised as Jews" (*Zummo* 1142). The trial court relied on David's oral agreement as grounds for awarding spiritual custody to Pamela (and stripping David of his rights). The judge maintained that he was not making a choice about the faith in which the children should be raised, but merely enforcing the parties' own agreement. In theory, this avoided the constitutional problem of having the court take sides in a religious controversy or infringe on the rights of parental autonomy, the idea being that the court was not taking a substantive position on the merits of the contending parents' faiths, but was merely giving effect to the substantive position that the parents themselves had long ago mutually reached.

But the court was taking a substantive position on the merits of competing theories about what children's best interests are. Using the contract argument enabled the trial court to side with the view that being exposed to more than one religion is psychologically painful and (what is not quite the same thing) actually harmful to children. It enabled the court (until it was reversed on appeal) to protect the children from the harms it perceived to flow from a "bi-cultural upbringing" without appearing to take a stand against the contrary view, put forth by David, that a bi-cultural upbringing was actually of positive benefit to the children. Instead, the court could fall back on the position that it was merely enforcing a contract, implementing the arrangement that the parents had mutually agreed upon – conveniently ignoring the fact that the argument for applying contract logic to spiritual custody disputes rests heavily on the view that a bi-cultural upbringing, with its attendant features of instability, inconsistency, and conflict, is not in the best psychological interests of children.

But in fact this is a disputable – and indeed disputed – view of children's needs and interests, although in today's climate, it may seem almost inconceivable that anyone could argue the contrary position. How could it possibly be that conflict, inconsistency, and instability are ever in a child's best interests? It is one thing to contend, as David Zummo did, that a "bi-cultural" upbringing is a positive good, but quite another to argue that conflict, inconsistency, and instability are of benefit to children. But once we get past the level of slogans, it seems undeniable that a bi-cultural upbringing in situations like the Zummos' necessarily entails some degree of conflict, inconsistency, and instability for the children. If we want to understand what children actually experience in situations like this, we have to get past comforting cultural bromides like "bi-culturalism" and dig out the constituent elements that a bi-cultural upbringing actually consists of: beliefs and practices that are sometimes antithetical to each other, as in the case of Judaism and Catholicism; belief-systems which pose a real threat of destabilizing or undermining each other; family cultures hostile towards each other; and divided loyalties to parents with different, sometimes contradictory expectations. Surely, Pamela wasn't wrong in sensing that allowing David to do what he wanted posed a real risk of undermining the children's attachment to Judaism and weakening their sense of Jewish identity. Under these circumstances, is it possible to doubt the conventional psychological wisdom that holds that children are better off being raised in one religious (or secular) culture?

It would take an act of sheer audacity, if not perversity, to argue against the view that instability and conflict are contrary to the best interests of children. Yet that is exactly what Judge Kelly did in the *Zummo* case, and his argument, once stated, seems anything but perverse. Indeed, once fully absorbed, it seems less audacious than commonsensical, albeit a version of common sense that contemporary popular culture has largely lost sight of. Kelly's point is simply this: "stress is not always harmful, nor is it always to be avoided and protected against." Acknowledging that "for children of divorce in general, and children of intermarriage and divorce especially, exposure to parents' conflicting values, lifestyles, and religious beliefs may indeed cause doubts and stress," Judge Kelly went on to say that "the key is not whether the child experiences stress, but whether the stress is unproductively severe." Short of that, claims of emotional harm are not sufficient to justify court intervention in parental religious disputes, and the principle of non-intervention must therefore be adopted.

Judge Kelly actually resisted the conventional psychological wisdom about the virtues of a consistent upbringing on several grounds. First, he observed that there is a "problem of causation" – that is, it is always hard to tell, when a child is distressed, if the suffering is actually caused by the religious upbringing dispute rather than by something else. It might well be that the child is suffering simply because "the parents have divorced or because of other factors unrelated to the religious upbringing issue." In a similar vein, Judge Kelly noted that claims about the psychological distress caused by exposure to more than one religious tradition are generally just conjectures, notwithstanding the psychological "experts" commonly brought in to testify in support of such claims. Following the lead of other courts, Judge Kelly rejected "speculation by parents and by experts" as being simply too speculative a basis on which to intervene in parental disputes in the name of protecting children from harm (*Zummo* 1155, 1156).

Both of these arguments go to the question of whether conflicting approaches to religion within a family really cause children harm. Judge Kelly cited the work of several scholars who have concluded that "exposing a child to more than one religion in the various households to which [the child] is attached does not, by itself, cause [the child] emotional stress or identity confusion" (Petsonk & Remsen 298; Mayer 42-45; Frideres, Goldstein & Gilbert 288-75; Schneidner 131; Heller 141-56; Rosenberg, Meehan & Payne 132-43; Cowan & Cowan 127-65, 255-62; Gruzen 62-63; Doyle 83-84).

But Judge Kelly's most powerful argument accepted the possibility that exposing impressionable children to multiple traditions can cause psychological stress and confusion. What he refused to do was make an elision between such psychological pain and harm. Again, "stress is not always harmful" (*Zummo* 1156). In fact, stress may best be regarded as an un-eliminable, essential, and even positive component of emotional and psychological development. "The process of a child's maturation requires that they view and evaluate their parents in the bright light of reality," Judge Kelly opined. "Children who learn their parents' weaknesses and strengths," he went on, "may be better able to shape life-long relationships with them." Therefore, he concluded, "courts ought not impose restrictions which unnecessarily shield children from the true nature of their parents unless it can be shown that some detrimental impact will flow from the specific behavior of the parent" – leading again to his favored position of non-intervention (*Zummo* 1155).

Thus, Judge Kelly dispensed with the automatic equation of harm with stress and conflict. As for the argument equating psychological harm with instability and change, Judge Kelly argued that "we are compelled ... to expressly disavow the suggestion ... that governmental interests in maintaining stability in spiritual inculcation exist which could provide a justification to encroach upon constitutionally recognized parental authority and First Amendment Free Exercise rights of a parent to attempt to inculcate religious beliefs in their children" (*Zummo* 1150). Acknowledging the "genuine comfort and reassurance a child *may* derive from *any* religion in a time of turmoil like divorce," Judge Kelly made the wry observation that "stability in a path to damnation could not be said to be more in a child's 'best interests' than an instability which offered the hope of movement toward a path to eternal salvation." Alluding to more skeptical views of religion, he noted as yet another possibility the theory that "all religions or a particular religion [are] merely harmful and repressive delusion," in which case "stability in such a delusion could not be said to be more in a child's 'best interests' than instability which might pave the way to escape from the delusion." The existence of such diverse views, as Judge Kelly saw it, only reinforces the case for non-intervention. "Because government cannot presume to have any knowledge as to which if any religions offer such eternal rewards or repressive delusions," Judge Kelly concluded, "the government simply cannot constitutionally prefer stability in religious beliefs to instability" (*Zummo* 1150).

For Judge Kelly, these arguments rejecting the equations commonly drawn between stress, confusion, conflict, and instability, on the one hand, and psychological harm, on the other, served to refute both the best interests approach, followed by many courts, and the contractualist approach, which, as we have seen, implicitly rests on the common best interests analysis. The best interests approach justifies judicial intervention in spiritual custody disputes, regardless of the existence of a prior spiritual custody agreement. It counsels deciding whether or not to grant the exclusive rights of spiritual custody to a parent on the basis of an open-ended inquiry into whether or not that outcome would be in the best interests of the child. The best interests inquiry is typically guided by the common assumptions regarding children's psychological interests in stability and consistency that were discussed above. In this now familiar view, anything that generates a sense of confusion or conflict is a kind of emotional harm that children have a right to be protected from. It is but a short step from this general proposition to the conclusion that courts must step in to protect children from the confusion and conflicts inherent in a bi-cultural upbringing. But once this general proposition is undermined, the argument that courts should make spiritual custody awards for the sake of the children crumbles.

With the best-interests argument weakened, the contractualist argument also loses one of its principal props. The question remains, however, why spiritual custody agreements should not be enforced, if not for the sake of the children, then for the sake of the general principles of freedom of contract and freedom of choice, which underlie ordinary contract law. If David Zummo, and others like him, freely entered into such contracts and made commitments of their own volition, why shouldn't they be held to them, as a matter of the basic principles of liberalism? Why should they be allowed to wriggle out of their commitments, especially given the seriousness of the stakes for everyone involved?

Judge Kelly took on this more fundamental contractualist argument on both narrow grounds of contract law doctrine, and on the grounds of general constitutional principles. As a matter of the technicalities of contract law, Judge Kelly argued that most spiritual custody agreements, like the oral commitment made by David Zummo, fail to satisfy the basic legal requirements for creating enforceable contracts. The terms of the agreement are simply too "indefinite" and "too vague to demonstrate a meeting of minds, or to provide an adequate basis for objective enforcement." Before they married, David and Pamela indeed made an agreement to raise their children as Jews. But, Judge Kelly observed, they "not surprisingly" had different understandings of the meaning of this commitment. Pamela envisioned "intense and exclusive Jewish religious indoctrination with exposure to only the most secular aspects of the father's Italian/Catholic heritage." David envisioned "that his children would receive formal Jewish education, [but] he did not understand it to preclude him from exposing the children to Catholic mass and other aspects of his cultural and religious heritage on a periodic basis" (*Zummo* 1145). Given these divergent understandings, which are quite typical in spiritual custody disputes, there *is* no mutual agreement, no "meeting of the minds," to be enforced.

Judge Kelly also made a more general case against enforcing spiritual custody contracts. Here, his argument referred not to the vagueness and indefiniteness of the terms of the agreement, but rather to the notion that unforeseeable changes in circumstances are not appropriately governed by contracts. This, too, is a standard contract law doctrine. But Judge Kelly applied the changed circumstances doctrine of contract law in a way that expressed a particular vision of the meaning of the principles of the constitution, a vision that forms the boldest and most distinctive part of his opinion.

And here we come to the core of his opinion: Spiritual custody awards, he argued, should not be granted on the basis of prior agreements between a couple because "such agreements generally will not be able to anticipate the fundamental changes in circumstances between their prenuptial optimism, their struggles for accommodation, and their ultimate post-divorce disillusionment." In short, in Judge Kelly's description, such agreements are hopelessly "hopeful" (one might better say, wishful) and "naive" – not, Judge Kelly suggests, because the couples who make them and break them are any more naive than the rest of us, but because the circumstances of romantic commitment have naivete, as it were, built into them. It would therefore be inappropriate, Judge Kelly goes on to argue, for courts to accept to enforce them, Judge Kelly. We no longer enforce wedding vows either, Judge Kelly reminds us, marriage being another arena where the value of "freedom from," embodied in the right to divorce, has been at least as fully recognized as the value of "freedom of" (*Zummo* 1147). And, if the marriage contract itself can be abrogated, why should a spiritual custody agreement be enforced?

Judge Kelly's argument here returns us to our original comparison of marriage and religion – and serial monogamy and serial faith – in the American popular imagination. Judge Kelly's opinion expresses a distinctive vision of the meaning and nature of freedom that is deeply rooted in American culture and popular religion. It is a distinctively liberal vision, but one that differs from other, perhaps more common understandings of liberalism, such as that which informs ordinary contract law doctrines. The liberal vision which Judge Kelly articulates gives pride of place not to the values of freedom of contract and commitment, but rather, to "the freedom to question, to doubt, and to change one's convictions." In Judge Kelly's interpretation, *these* are the core values enshrined in the First Amendment. Insisting that "religious development is a lifelong dynamic process even for people who continue to adhere to the same religion, denomination or sect," Judge Kelly gave voice to a vision of religous and personal freedom that emphasizes liberal (or what one might call, following the legal theorist Roberto Unger, "super-liberal") values of dynamism, transformation, and ongoing change, as against the inherently conservative values of stability and contractual obligation (*Zummo* 1146).

Such a dynamic understanding of freedom, centered on the right to change, reveals the essential link between "freedom of" or "freedom to" and "freedom from" or "freedom not to." For change always implies both a movement away from a former status quo, and a movement towards a new one. The right to change is, by definition, perpetual, or, in the more common language of liberal rights, "inalienable," and for that very reason, not to be conveyed away by contract, like some sort of material good. As Judge Kelly explained:

> The First Amendment specifically preserves the essential religious freedom for individuals to grow, to shape, and to amend this important aspect of their lives, and the lives of their children. Religious freedom was recognized by our founding fathers to be *inalienable*. It remains so today. Thus, while we agree that a parent's religious freedom may yield to other compelling interests, we conclude that it may be bargained away (*Zummo* 1148).

This, of course, is the same dynamic understanding of personal development that has come to prevail in the area of the law of marriage and divorce, where we have elevated the freedom to change one's mind (or one's heart) over the value of unbreakable commitments. (It was Milton who penned the first great liberal argument for the right to divorce, based on the right to changes of heart, in the name of deeply religious Christian conception of liberty and love.) (Milton). Indeed, it appears that in the domain of marriage, we have come to tolerate almost unlimited amounts of conflict and change, whereas only in the context of custody proceedings are changes of religious faith and religious conflicts between parents expected to be legally contained and subdued. As Judge Kelly noted, it is an anomaly that we permit spiritual custody disputes to take place between parents who are married to each other, virtually without restraint, and only subject parents who are not married to each other to judicial intervention (*Zummo* 1140).

Of course, the normative implications of the anomalous treatment of marriage could cut either way. One could just as well make the case for judicial intervention in "healthy marriages," as argue against making spiritual custody awards in cases of divorce, if the sole concern is consistency. It is only Judge Kelly's emphasis on the value of the right to "grow," "amend," and change in the religious sphere that makes it clear which way the anomaly has to cut. The right to divorce represents the triumph of the dynamic understanding of liberalism, centered on the freedom to change, over more conservative notions of stabilizing contracts and commitments. So too, does the right to diverge from one's spouse, or former spouse, or even from one's former self when it comes to the religious upbringing of one's children.

This dynamic vision of liberalism is what ultimately led Judge Kelly to reject the judicial award of spiritual custody to one parent on any grounds, be it the children's supposed best interests, or the parents' supposed agreement. If Judge Kelly is correct in holding that the First Amendment protects the "constitutional freedom to question, to doubt, and to change one's convictions," then there is never any basis for enforcing an exclusive right to control the children's upbringing against another parent, save for the extreme situation where a parent's religious practices threaten a child with actual, serious harm. As a general rule, non-intervention logically follows from this vision of personal freedom, centered on a right of perpetual change.

There are two great ironies to Judge Kelly's opinion. The first, already alluded to, is that this principle of non-intervention is subject to much the same critique that he made of the contractualist and best-interests approaches. While seeking to preserve both Pamela's and David's freedom of religion, the decision in *Zummo v. Zummo* inevitably gave full protection to only one parent's right to "shape this important aspect of their lives, and the lives of their children," while limiting the other's. David was in effect given free rein to give his children the "bi-cultural upbringing" he valued, while Pamela had to submit to input from David that cut against her desire for an exclusively Jewish upbringing. Judge Kelly's decision was no more neutral, in this respect, than any other. And it seems that there is simply no escaping from this dilemma of neutrality.

The other great irony of Judge Kelly's opinion is that, while it honors the general principle of the separation of church and state enshrined in the First Amendment's establishment clause, the vision it gives voice to is actually, in terms of its origins, a deeply religious one. More particularly, it derives from a specifically

Protestant tradition of valuing religious conversion experiences as the quintessential expression of religious commitment and choice. Conversion experiences have always had a special place in America's popular religious culture, thanks to the particular combination of Christian and Romanticist ideas that shaped American culture. From its Puritan beginnings, an American culture of "personal growth" and "religious freedom" has always invited individuals to consider embarking on new "spiritual journeys" and undergoing "changes of faith." Far from being a phenomenon unique to the inter-faith marriage situation, the possibility of transforming one's religious identity has long been regarded, and valorized, as a standing possibility for everyone, at any time.

Of course, there has never been any guarantee that one person's "spiritual growth" would proceed in lockstep with another's. Protestant lore is full of stories, like that of Christian in John Bunyan's The Pilgrim's Progress, whose journey to Jesus required that he leave his domestic hearth with his fingers stopped in his ears in order to prevent his being lured back by the cries of his wife and his children. The religious-romanticist tradition has always recognized that the freedom of the spirit necessitates breaking earthly commitments, in particular the commitments we make as a parent and as a spouse. Unlike some contemporary versions of liberalism, particularly those inflected with pop psychology, this religiously-rooted version of liberalism has never pretended that spiritual freedom is easy or conflict-free.

Over time, this Christian-Romantic conception of religion and religious freedom has steadily become secularized. We can recognize many of the elements of the originally Protestant conception of spiritual growth present in the contemporary theories of psychological development that shape our popular attitudes today. By the same token, religious denominations other than Protestantism have assumed many of its guiding values and reformed themselves in its image – not only the various non-Protestant denominations of Christianity, but non-Christian religions, such as Judaism, as well. In particular, the motifs of spiritual growth, and the concomitant right to changes of heart and mind, recur today in all major American religious denominations.

From this perspective, the final irony may be that parents coming from different religious backgrounds clash at all, given the cultural convergence of all of the major American religious denominations on the values of religious freedom, spiritual growth, conversion, and the right to change. But the same spirit of individuality that gives you the freedom to embark upon a new spiritual journey means you can never be certain if your partner is along for the ride. In fact, given our commitment to the individuality of religious experience, it is likely that one partner's "spiritual" evolution is going to differ in more or less significant ways from the other's. Even when both partners start and finish as members of the same religious denomination, even when both partners are secular and consistently shun religious affiliations, in the absence of legal mechanisms that subordinate one parent to the authority of another, as in the patriarchal days of yore, some differences over their children's "spiritual" development are bound to occur, belying the myth of the culturally homogeneous family.

These, then, are the lessons of *Zummo v. Zummo*. In the words of a recent advice book to couples: *"every marriage is a mixed marriage"* (Stoner 20).

And everyone is born and raised in spiritual custody. There is no escape from spiritual custody, because even the most "liberal" of parents imposes a particular upbringing on their children, and even bi- or multi-cultural families transmit a particular culture – namely, the culture of multiculturalism. There is no such thing as "mere exposure," because exposure to competing points of view always shapes the children who are exposed in distinctive ways – ways different from those of a more insulated culture. Being exposed to more than one religious tradition takes certain choices away, at the same time that it opens up others. The same is true of being raised in a homogenous culture.

These lessons help to explain the basic conundrum of religion's vulnerability in a liberal society, with which we began. Religious affiliations *are* vulnerable in a liberal society; liberalism *does* threaten to disrupt the chain of cultural transmission from one generation to the next, as statistics on assimilation and secularization bear out. But what religious affiliations are vulnerable to – what it is that threatens to disrupt the chain of transmission is not precisely choice. Religious affiliations cannot be said to be entirely voluntary once we recognize the powerful forces of socialization and acculturation that are always at play in families in the form of "spiritual custody." What religious traditions are vulnerable to, as the case of *Zummo v. Zummo* shows, is not so much choice as each other.

In *Zummo*, it was David's religious tradition that threatened to undermine Pamela's (and vice verse) – not some detached faculty of free choice that the children would somehow magically come into possession of at the age of majority. In fact, David and Pamela's children were destined to be shaped by their experiences, and by the control exercised over them by both parents (as are we all). If the effect of the decision would be to lead them away from the Jewish identity that Pamela (and David) intended for them – and there is no predicting what the outcome would be – that would not be the result of their having escaped the common fate of being subject to cultural conditioning by one's parents, but rather, of having had the right to cultural conditioning by both parents guaranteed. It is not the absence, but rather, the *surfeit* of cultural conditioning that might – and one wants to emphasize only *might* – end up disposing the children against their mother's (or their father's) religious heritage. Conflict, then, not choice, appears to be the essential catalyst of religious transformation. Or to put it another way, conflict is the catalyst of choice – not the other way around.

Works Cited

Black, James C. and Donald J. Cantor. Child Custody. New York: Columbia UP, 1989.

Cowan, Paul and Rachel Cowan. Mixed Blessings. New York: Doubleday, 1987.

Dailey, Anne C. "Federalism and Families." University of Pennsylvania Law Review 143 (1995): 1787-1888.

Doyle. "The Roman Catholic Church and Mixed Marriages" Ecumenical Trends 14 (1985): 81.

Ellis, Sarah Strickney. The Women of England: Their Social Duties and Domestic Habits. London, 1839.

Fineman, Martha. "Dominant Discourse, Professional Language, and Legal Change in Child Custody Decision Making." Harvard Law Review 101 (1988): 727-774.

Freeman, Lauren D. "The Child's Best Interests vs. The Parent's Free Exercise of Religion." Columbia Journal of Law and Social Problems 32 (1998): 73-97.

Frideres, Goldstein & Gilbert 288-75 "The Impact of Jewish-Gentile Intermarriages in Canada." Journal of Comparative Family Studies 2 (1971): 268.

Gregory, John Dewitt. "Family Privacy and the Custody and Visitation Rights of Adult Outsiders." Family Law Quarterly 36 (2002): 163-187.

Gruzen, Lee F. Raising Your Jewish/Christian Child: Wise Choice for Interfaith Parents. Dodd Mead, 1987.

Guttman, Amy. Democratic Education. Princeton: Princeton UP, 1987.

Hackett v. Hackett. 146 N.E.2d 477. OH Com. Pl. 1957.

Kandel, Randy Frances. Family Law: Essential Terms and Concepts. New York: Aspen, 2000.

Macedo, Stephen. Diversity and Distrust: Civic Education in a Multicultural Democracy. Cambridge: Harvard UP, 2000.

Mayer, Egon. Love and Tradition: Marriage Between Jews and Christians. New York: Schocken, 1985.

Petsonk, Judy and Jim Remsen. The Intermarriage Handbook: A Guide for Jews and Christians. New York: Quill, 1988.

Rosenberg, Rabbi Roy A., Father Peter Meehan, and John W. Payne. Happily Intermarried: Authoratative Advice for a Happy Jewish/ Christian Marriage. New York: Crowell-Collier, 1989.

Sandel, Michael. "The Procedural Republic and the Unencumbered Self." Political Theory 12 (1984): 81.

Stoner, Carroll. Weddings for Grownups: Everything That You Need to Know to Plan Your Wedding. San Francisco: Chronicle, 1997.

Strauber, Jocelyn E. "A Deal Is a Deal: Antenuptial Agreements Regarding Religious Upbringing of Our Children Should Be Enforceable." Duke Law Journal 47 (1998): 971-1012.

Walzer, Michael. "The Communitarian Critique of Liberalism." Political Theory 18 (1990): 6.

Zummo v. Zummo. 574 A.2d 1130. PA Super. Ct. 1990.

Chapter Two

CULTURE:
What Price Success? Materialism in American Jewish Drama

By Ted Merwin

Yiddish, to most Americans, is fun. Even non-Jews occasionally use Yiddish words, eat Yiddish foods and enjoy music and humor inflected with a Yiddish sensibility. And American Jews are justifiably proud of the ways Eastern-European Jewish culture has been incorporated into American culture. Almost every year, for example, another book is published listing the Yiddish words that have entered American English – many of them starting with a "sch" sound: e.g., schmooze, schmuck, schlep.[1] Traditional Jewish foods like bagels, pastrami and matzoh balls have become part of the general American cuisine. Klezmer music ("Jewish jazz") is frequently heard on radio, film and television. And

---

[1] The title of a recent popular book of walking tours, with no Jewish subtext whatsoever, is *Washington Schlepped Here*.

comedians like Jackie Mason and Fran Drescher, both of whom speak with heavy New York-Jewish accents, are successful mainstream entertainers.

It was not always thus. When Jews fleeing persecution first began to flood the shores of the East Coast around the turn of the last century, they were treated as outcasts. Earlier immigrant Jews from Germany, through their success in merchandising and finance, had already begun to make a mark. However, the influx of Eastern-European Jews was seen as threatening to the very fabric of American society. They were stigmatized for their peculiar-sounding language and family names, their lack of English fluency and seeming deficiency of good taste in dress and grooming.

Vaudeville comedians would dress up as long-nosed, long-bearded Jews and mock them – to howls of laughter from predominantly non-Jewish audiences. Early silent films showed Jews as conniving moneylenders and dishonest businessmen, often setting their own stores on fire to collect insurance payments. But Yiddish-speaking Jews quickly made a mark on American society. Ironically, the very immigrants who were so derided for their Old World attire became identified with the nascent ready-made clothing industry – particularly women's clothing – and had a large influence on setting fashion trends for the country.[2]

This genius for self-promotion was nowhere more evident than in the entertainment business, where Jewish movie moguls helped to create a much more sympathetic image of the Jew than the one propagated by non-Jews. By the second generation, Jewish Americans were becoming significantly more accepted by other Americans, even as they largely continued to marry other Jews, work with other Jews, join synagogues and live in Jewish neighborhoods. The way Jews were represented in mainstream popular culture – radio, Broadway plays and films – played a large role in promoting more positive perceptions and images of Jews in American society.

Joining the mainstream, however, ultimately required

---

[2] Many immigrant Jewish clothing manufacturers were successful, notes Irving Howe, partly because they had a talent for advertising their lines to mainstream Americans (Howe 154).

renouncing ethnic particularism and clannishness. American society values both cultural diversity *and* cultural mixing. Still at the beginning of the 21st century, there remain very few native Yiddish speakers living in America, few Jewish delis – even in New York, where they once stood on almost every street corner – and only one professional Yiddish theater.

Thus the price of Jews' success in America has been, it is safe to say, the loss of much of what made them distinctive. Yet Jewish culture has also adapted to American life in creative ways, transforming both the ethnic subculture and the host society.

This essay focuses on the theater in particular as the locus of Jewish identity among early 20th-century Jewish immigrants. I will concentrate on a particular play, Osip Dymov's *Bronx Express,* as an example of the role that American Jews played in reconciling traditional, communal values with the individualistic values of American capitalism and consumerism. This play, along with other English-language plays about New York-Jewish life that followed it, demonstrates how Jews renegotiated the terms of both their collective and individual identities and set the stage (both literally and figuratively) for the fuller integration of Jews into American society.

The Origins of Yiddish Theater

Yiddish theater thrived for only about five decades, roughly from 1875 to 1925. As Nahma Sandrow has explained in her lively and informative history of Yiddish theater, *Vagabond Stars*, there was a strong prejudice against theater in traditional Jewish practice for thousands of years; theater was associated with cross-dressing, sexual immorality and the duplicity that comes with role-playing in general. This despite the fact that, as David Lifson has pointed out, Jewish rituals have always contained an element of theater (19).[3]

Even during the Renaissance, when European theater was reaching its artistic zenith, the only explicitly theatrical forms found in the Jewish communities of Eastern Europe were the

---

[3] For example, the dramatic way the Torah and other Jewish texts are chanted in synagogue, the role-playing elements of the Passover seder.

Purim plays – performed on the only Jewish festival that licensed the rowdiness associated with theatrical activity – and the often ribald clowning provided by wedding jesters, or *badkhonim*.

Yiddish had developed out of a medieval form of German called Middle High German, with bits of both European languages (especially French) and Slavic languages (especially Russian) mixed in. But for centuries it occupied an inferior place in Jewish culture compared to Hebrew; it was associated primarily with women and the home.[4] Hebrew, the sacred language of Jewish texts and synagogue liturgy, was the preserve of men. During the 18th-century Enlightenment, Jews began to move from *shtetlach* (market towns) to cities, and to participate in European intellectual and professional life. The *haskole*, or Jewish Enlightenment, emerged as an alternative to traditional religious Judaism, on the one hand, and to the newer movement known as Hasidism, whose followers believed in direct access to God through mystical practices and passionate song and dance. For followers of the *haskole,* known as *maskilim*, and for Hasidim alike, Yiddish was the authentic expression of folk culture that deserved its own literature.

Only in the 1870s, however, did a genuine Yiddish theater emerge. Avrom Goldfadn, a traveling folk singer, began writing plays attacking the inflexible religious customs and medieval superstitions of the traditionally pious Jews of his time. These plays – heavy on slapstick, farce and comic songs – were built around the personalities of the actors in Goldfadn's theater company, which he had founded in a wine cellar in Jassy, Romania. According to Sandrow, Goldfadn viewed himself as "weaning simple people out of cultural isolation into the non-Jewish world." The very fact that he used folk culture to do so, she argues, shows that Goldfadn was "actually entering and enriching popular tradition while he thought he was guiding his audience away from it" (Sandrow, "Vagabond Stars," 50). From its inception, Yiddish theater thus served dual contradictory purposes – widening the gap between traditional Jewish practice and the modern world,

---

[4] Hence the familiar term for Yiddish, *mameloshen*, or mother's tongue.

while solidifying the attachment that Jews felt to their native culture.

Yiddish Theater Crosses the Ocean

This was nowhere so true as in America. The millions of Jewish immigrants who came to these shores needed, even as they struggled to learn English and make their way in a foreign country, the social and emotional bonds that Yiddish theater provided. The theater served much the same function that the synagogue had done in the Old Country, providing a public space in which immigrants could gather. But since the time of the ancient Greeks, theater has been fundamental to the life of the community in a more abstract sense: as a place for exploring and remaking myths and communal self-understandings. Jewish immigrants used the theater as a way to interpret their own experience of being strangers in a strange land and take comfort by working through their feelings of alienation as part of a community.

Yiddish theater was always dominated more by the outsize performances of its actors than by its texts.[5] The texts are also important, however, in understanding how Yiddish culture developed in America and how Jews remade Jewish life in an American context.

The first period of American-Yiddish theater was marked by extravagant operettas about Jewish history, many of them set in ancient Palestine. These were written principally by two dramatists: Joseph Lateiner and Moshe Hurwitz. Both were play "bakers," hacks who banged out a play a week by stealing scenes, characters, and even entire plotlines from other plays to feed the Lower East Side's ravenous appetite for Yiddish entertainment. Hurwitz's and Lateiner's plays perhaps "served no worthwhile ideas" and "were popular [only] because the immigrant masses responded to melodrama" (Lifson 77). But Jewish immigrants no doubt were glad to be reminded of the glory of their history – whether accurately presented or not – as they struggled to make

---

[5] Among the most famous Yiddish actors were Jacob Adler, Joseph Buloff, Bertha Kalish, David Kessler and Boris Thomashevsky.

their way in a culture that had little respect for Jews. And what better way to assuage feelings of dislocation than a play about the Jewish homeland? For even as immigrants saw America as a kind of "promised land," there was little evidence that this place could ever be home.

Other popular genres of plays were *tsaytbilder*, or "scenes of the times"; sensationalistic plays on current events, like murders and natural disasters; and domestic melodramas about family conflicts, in which the romantic freedom of American life contrasts with the traditional Jewish ways of Eastern Europe. Immigrant family life tended to be chaotic: large numbers of husbands deserted their families; children often rejected the ways of their parents. So these plays about family life often spoke to real crises that audience members were experiencing.

They also set the stage for the emergence of Jacob Gordin, a playwright who brought an intellectual tone to Yiddish theater. He sought to invest Yiddish theater with the realism that characterized late 19th-century European drama, then dominated by Ibsen, Strindberg and Chekhov. Gordin brought psychological complexity to his characters and used his plays to explore changing social conditions in the tenements, sweatshops and immigrant relief organizations that the audience knew first-hand.

Gordin was also very successful in adapting Shakespeare. For example, his *Jewish King Lear* (1892), set in Lithuania, focused on a businessman who, wishing to emigrate to Palestine, divides his estate among three adult daughters. But the play really explores how different kinds of Jews are forced to adapt to the modern world and its economic and social arrangements. The audience "may be uprooted, poor and struggling to understand their new surroundings," writes Joel Berkowitz, "but – Gordin suggests – if they cast off the worst of the old ways and embrace the best of the new, they will succeed in the New World" (Berkowitz 49). Gordin's play, while pedantic, tried to teach immigrants that the conflict between Jewish values and American values could only be resolved by giving up the former in exchange for the latter.

With the prosperity that followed World War I, Jews migrated out of the ghetto into the newer Jewish neighborhoods of the Bronx and Brooklyn. Yiddish theater moved with them. But turning its back on realism, it flexed its artistic muscles in new ways. Playwrights experimented with freer conceptions of stage time and space, spurred to some extent by the avant-garde movements prevalent in Europe – surrealism, expressionism, constructivism and so forth.[6]

Director and impresario Maurice Schwartz was the most influential proponent of an "art" theater moving in a non-realistic direction.[7] Irving Howe has called this period "the last major upsurge of Yiddish theater in America" (485). Among the most successful of this new breed of play was one by Russian-Jewish playwright Osip Dymov; it used the New York subway as a metaphor for the journey Jews embarked upon in entering American society.

Subway To Heaven – Or Hell?

Dymov's *Bronks Ekspres (Bronx Express)* opened on December 31, 1919, in New York's Naye Yidishe Teater (New Jewish Theatre). The author, whose original name was Yosef Perlman (1878-1959), was a successful Russian playwright whose works had been translated into Polish, German and Hebrew.[8] *Bronks Ekspres* is one of his best-known works. Directed originally by the celebrated actor Jacob Ben-Ami and Dymov himself, this Faust story deals with the head-on collision between Old World values and the American way.

The play's central character is Khatskl Hungershtolts ("Harry Hungerproud"), an immigrant button-maker who has moved his family to the Bronx, but continues to work on the Lower East Side. In the prologue, he is traveling home one evening when he meets an old friend, Yankl Flyamkes ("Jake Flames"), on the subway. Flyamkes describes the glamorous world of

---

[6] European companies like the Vilna Troupe, which toured the United States, also inspired a host of imitators.

[7] Among the playwrights to work with Schwartz and his Yiddish Art Theatre were Peretz Hirschbein (*Green Fields*), H. Leivick (*The Golem*), S. Anski (*The Dybbuk*), and Osip Dymov (*The Awakening of a Folk*).

[8] He only started writing in Yiddish after he came to America in 1913. (His name is sometimes spelled "Dymow." His other plays include *Yoshke Musikant [Yoshke the Musician]*, 1914, and *Di Ervakhung fun a Folk [The Awakening of a People]*, 1921.)

manufacturing and high finance. Poking fun at Hungershtolts's loyalty to family and faith, Flyamkes turns to the fictional characters adorning the advertising posters for consumer products – Aunt Jemima, the Nestlé Baby, the Smith Brothers (of Smith Brothers Cough Drops) and so on.[9] Flyamkes touts the millions of dollars these "people" have earned, and tempts Hungershtolts to sell himself, his wife and the entire Jewish people for money. In Act I, Flyamkes visits Hungershtolts' home in the outer borough neighborhood of Bronx Park, where the family is eating Sabbath dinner. Hungershtolts decides to abandon them and go off with Flyamkes. Act II takes place at the mansion of the "Mr. Pluto Corporation."[10] Here Hungershtolts meets the characters from the subway advertisements, magically come to life; he falls in love with Miss Murad, a harem girl representing Turkish cigarettes. Act III finds Hungershtolts in Atlantic City, married to Miss Murad. She has given birth to the Nestlé Baby, whom he pushes in a carriage. Hungershtolts' deserted family shows up; his daughter is romanced by one of the Smith Brothers. Tormented by pangs of conscience, Hungershtolts tries to drown himself but he is saved by Flyamkes. When Hungershtolts' first wife accuses him of bigamy, he begs to return to his former life. As the Pluto devil prepares to lynch him for his misdeeds, Hungershtolts wakes up on the subway. The whole episode has been a nightmare.

Despite his name, Hungershtolts takes pride not so much in being poor as in being Jewish. He has taken in his old religious school teacher, he reads the Yiddish newspaper, he celebrates the Sabbath and Jewish holidays with his family, and he enjoys his favorite Jewish foods. Flyamkes, the renegade Jew, scorns these relationships and activities. He accuses Hungershtolts of living a meaningless life, of "sleeping through America, and under America" rather than participating in the world of money-making.

The subway is a metaphorical Hell from which Flyamkes (clearly modeled on Mephistopheles from Goethe's *Faust*) dissociates himself; he invites Hungershtolts to the realm of the

---

[9] The names are transliterated into Yiddish in the original text. English words are common in American-Yiddish drama, since they reflect the acculturation of Jewish characters.
[10] Mascot of Pluto Mineral Water, represented by a devil with a red tail.

Bronx Express. (L to R) Victor Packer, John Bleifer, Vera Lebeder, Rudolph Schildkraut.
Photographer: White Studio
Rudolph Schildkraut Theatre, the Bronx, 1925
Museum of the City of New York Theater Collection / Gift of John Bleifer

"high windows" on Wall Street and Fifth Avenue. But
Hungershtolts cannot imagine what he could sell to make money;
he owns nothing of material value. Flyamkes' suggests: "buttons,
cotton, silk, milk, yourself, your wife, your people" (Sandrow
"Bronx Express" 272). In the capitalist marketplace, everything
is for sale.

Hungershtolts buys stock over the telephone from John D.
Rockefeller, and calls President Calvin Coolidge to talk business.
In a conversation with the Pluto devil, he realizes how he can
most effectively betray his people: he will make them work on
their most sacred holiday.

> HUNGERSHTOLTS: Make an agreement with all the
> shops, all the factories, downtown, uptown, that day
> they pay the Jews double, triple, ten times. They'll work
> Yom Kippur too.
>
> PLUTO: Jews love money.

HUNGERSHTOLTS: Sure, Jews love money. This one has a sick child and has to buy medicine. That one has an old father or mother or just an old rebbe who can't work but wants to eat anyway, or a wife exhausted in the kitchen from hard work. Or relatives in misery back home. Yes, yes, Jews do love money. They'll work Yom Kippur too.

PLUTO: Go on, go on.

HUNGERSHTOLTS: Yom Kippur breaks down, everything breaks down. No holidays, no religion, no tradition, one big pot of schmaltz. Everyone cooked in the same pot. The iron grinder grinds them all up together, with the Poles, Italians, Chinese, Japanese, Negroes – everything thrown in the iron wheels. Wheels and people – a machine with no holidays, no language, no traditions – a great mass of workers that works and buys, works and buys, and eats, and chews, and swallows. Two for a quarter, five for a dozen. The nicest, the best, delicious, you need it. Historical process, capital and labor (Sandrow "Bronx Express" 294-295).

Pluto is so enraptured with the idea that he asks for the rights to it; when Hungershtolts refuse, Miss Murad distracts him with a lustful dance and Pluto gets Hungershtolts to "sign" by moving his hand over the paper. The betrayal of the Jews is complete.[11]

The idea of the melting pot was, of course, not new. It was the Anglo-Jewish writer Israel Zangwill whose play *The Melting Pot*, first performed in Washington, D.C. in 1908, popularized what became a very influential idea in American culture. The immigrant Jewish hero of that play, violinist David Quixano, sees the melting pot as the crucible in which the hatreds and antagonisms of the Old World are burned away – like dross refined into gold. In Zangwill's play, the melting pot is an agent for the

---

[11] The linchpin of Jewish identity is seen as the Day of Atonement, when Jews are supposed to seek forgiveness for their sins.

regeneration of mankind.

Dymov's take on the metaphor is strikingly different; he satirizes the melting pot as a big pot of *schmaltz*, the chicken fat in which many traditional Eastern-European Jewish foods were cooked. The idea that Yom Kippur, a holiday when Jews fast, is to be a day for infernal "cooking" only adds to the sacrilege. Dymov's perspective is unabashedly socialistic. Jews will become indistinguishable from other ethnic groups, and all Americans will become animalistic engines for consumption. The loss of religion will remove from Jews what makes them Jewish and detach from all Americans what makes them human. The soul-less machine will destroy the souls of American workers.

The Evils of Capitalism

Dymov's surrealistic play focuses on how both workers and products circulate in a modern capitalist economy. The horizontal motion of the train seems counterbalanced by the vertical distance between the terrestrial and supernatural realms. Hungershtolts is so seduced by capitalist values that he loses his grip on reality. "Novelists and politicians agreed in describing the [1920s] as an entrepreneurial riot," wrote Stephen Fox. "Advertising reached its apogee when it became hard to distinguish between real life and ad life" (Fox 79).

The contrast between reality and fantasy is a major theme of *Bronks Ekspres*. Indeed, by using figures of American commerce as evil spirits, the play holds as many demons and devils as the popular Yiddish dramas of the Old Country.[12] Yet *Bronks Ekspres* also broke new ground on the Yiddish stage in terms of realism – with its exact replica of a subway car interior on the old White Plains Road line and its terminus in Bronx Park.

That the play created a strong impression of a world off kilter is clear from Boris Aronson's set and costume designs for a 1925 revival at the Unser Theatre in the Bronx.[13] The ceiling of the

---

[12] Plays like Jacob Gordin's *Got, Mentsh, un Tayvl (God, Man and Devil*, 1900) and David Pinski's *Der Oytser (The Treasure*, 1906).

[13] The revival starred Rudolph Schildkraut as Hungershtolts and Victor Packer as the Pluto devil. The former, a movie star, appeared around the same time in the silent film *His People*, a melodrama about immigrant Jewish life. The latter was to achieve fame in the late 1930s and early 1940s as a radio programming director who read his own Dadaist poetry on the air and did "man-on-the-street interviews long before David Letterman made them popular.

subway train, with its hanging straps, remained on the set even as the surroundings changed. The demonic figures of American commerce – leering gargoyles lurching with the motion of the train – look like figures from a German expressionist film.[14]

Aronson's costumes, however, brought in an element of visual pleasure that softened the feel of the production. In fact, they were so brash and colorful that the star actor complained he had nothing to do; he was upstaged by his own costume (Rich 36)! By emphasizing the importance of packaging, the set and costume designs intensified Dymov's indictment of capitalism as a system based on surfaces and visual allure. The train had been a potent symbol of the industrial machine since Victorian times in both America and Europe; in *Bronks Ekspres* these associations were transferred from the manufacturing process to the marketing of the resulting consumer products.

As in other non-Yiddish plays of the 1920s that used expressionistic devices – such as Elmer Rice's *The Adding Machine* (1923) and Eugene O'Neill's *The Hairy Ape* (1922) – capitalist society in *Bronks Ekspres* robs the protagonist of his identity by detaching him from membership in a community. To some extent, as Simon Bronner has suggested, "the impression of a society of consumers raised images of breaking down the isolation of people. Shared goods meant having more in common; therefore, a scattered society still could be close even if it meant that strangers could hide behind the façade of their things" (Bronner 51).

While common products provided topics for conversation, consumers quickly found they could not substitute for older forms of community, in which objects were valued for the time and labor required to produce them. "By implying that basic human needs could be satisfied by consumption of the tangible products of modern industry," argues James Norris, "advertising exacerbated the conflict between the values of an older America and the realities of modern industrial society" (69). This was especially

---

[14] Films such as *Cabinet of Dr. Caligari* (1919). That the subway was taking on fearful connotations as early as the 1920s is evident from Elmer Rice's drama *The Subway* (1924), depicting the underground transit system as a frightening, claustrophobia-inducing symbol of both the speed of modern life and the threat of urban violence.

true for Jews, since many came from agrarian societies where mass-produced goods were unknown.

Yet capitalism seemed to undermine fixed entities of any kind. As Dymov perspicaciously recognized, the American industrial system makes the maintenance of a stable identity contingent on endless consumption – fueled by an insatiable need, instilled by advertisers, for new products. Tempting Hungershtolts to leave home and eat a non-kosher meal on Broadway, Flyamkes promises: "When you eat just one meal there, you'll realize that all your life you've been hungry" (Sandrow "Bronx Express" 279). This seems to be more than a jibe at the blandness of kosher food. Flyamkes implies that tasting American cuisine will reveal to Hungershtolts how unfulfilling his life has been in its slavish adherence to Jewish ritual.

Consumer goods were becoming substitutes for the care that other human beings had previously provided. As Bronner concluded from a study of late 19th-century novels: "The Victorian stuffed interior comforted guests so that human hands did not have to.... The easy offering of emotions through consumer goods allowed for a growing sense of restraint in human relations, which raised questions ... about the real meaning and feeling of facades in a consumer landscape of signs" (Bronner 52). Advertisements themselves came to imply the excitement and promise of America,[15] while masking the emotional and spiritual emptiness consumption left in its wake.

Jews and other immigrants came to America, of course, just as the American industrial economy was maturing; the lure of easy employment was what brought them here in the first place. William Leach writes that after the Civil War, "American capitalism began to produce a distinct culture, unconnected to traditional family or community values, to religion in any conventional sense, or to political democracy" (Leach 3). The basic features of this culture, according to Leach, are "acquisition and consumption as the means of achieving happiness; the cult of the new; the democratization of desire; and money as the

---

[15] Consider Times Square in Manhattan.

predominant measure of all value in society" (Leach 3). These values were clearly in conflict with Jewish tradition in many ways. This did not mean, as Gordin suggested in *Jewish King Lear*, that Jews had to choose between the two. Social historians have documented creative ways of merging Jewish values with American ones.

Creating Jewish Americans

Jenna Weissman Joselit argues that Jewish immigrants bought American products not to give up their Judaism but to create homes expressing their dual identities. According to Joselit, American Jews "shared an abiding, deeply felt belief in the intimate connection between Jewishness and domesticity." Shopping was "a tangible instrument of integration and Americanization," but also a way to celebrate Jewish culture in an American context (Joselit 5).

Yiddish newspapers actively promoted the purchase of mainstream merchandise by Jewish immigrants.[16] While the ads implied these products would help Jews become more American, the very fact of their being translated into Yiddish meant manufacturers were participating in Jewish culture – "Yiddishizing" themselves in order to reach out to Jewish immigrants.

Many of the advertisements were targeted at women, who did the bulk of the household shopping. Andrew Heinze points to a Yiddish newspaper ad for Fels Naptha soap.[17] The product is represented by the character of "Aunty Drudge," a homemaker with the highest standards of cleanliness and purity. Yet the campaign also incorporated images of a fashionably attired young woman, part of the advertising industry's emphasis on being "up-to-date" (Heinze "Jewish Women" 25). This made sense for Jewish immigrants, who were eager to shed their greenhorn status and join the American mainstream.

---

[16] In a study of Yiddish newspaper advertisements, Joselit found ads for Uneeda Biscuit, Gulden's Mustard, Colgate's Dental Cream, Eagle Brand Condensed Milk, Community Silver, Chevrolet and Dutch Master Cigars – among many others.

[17] The product of a Jewish soap manufacturer.

To be sure, Jews reached the lower-middle class partly by buying the clothes, house wares, furnishings, musical instruments and other symbols of middle-class life. According to Heinze, who applies Thorsten Veblen's theories about "conspicuous consumption" to Jewish immigrant buying patterns, the newcomers "relied on their awareness of the symbolic potential of special products as they searched for a tangible American identity" (Heinze "Adapting…" 223). Immigrants vied to be as "up-to-date" as possible by acquiring the accoutrements of an Americanized identity.

An emphasis on consumption transformed even Jewish religious observance. Ready access to higher-quality food throughout the week made Sabbaths and holidays – when families had traditionally eaten delicacies, like chicken, and consumed special beverages, like seltzer – seem more ordinary. Many Jews felt compelled to work on Saturdays to support their families. As the boundaries between religious and secular activity began to dissolve, it became harder to tell them apart. This gave birth to an American-Jewish culture.

Sweatshop Plays

The Yiddish press received *Bronks Ekspres* enthusiastically. The original production fell into none of the clearly defined categories of Yiddish theater: it was not operetta, vaudeville, comedy or drama, commented Abraham Cahan, editor of the influential newspaper *Forvertz* (Forward). Yet it was both "original" and "interesting," and the author was brimming with "juice." The play, Cahan added, was well-acted from top to bottom (5).

While few Yiddish plays were translated into English, *Bronks Ekspres* seemed to producer Charles Coburn to have potential for success on Broadway. Adapted by Owen Davis and translated into English by Samuel Golding, it opened on April 26, 1922, at the Astor Theatre. Golding's translation changed the play in some respects. For example, in addition to inducing the Jewish workers to renounce Yom Kippur, Hungershtolts decides that he and the Pluto devil should contrive the "Americanization of all the foreigners," meaning not just Jewish holidays, but all ethnic holidays should be eliminated: "No more Columbus Day! No more Good Friday! No more St. Patrick's Day! Let them work on the holidays" (Dymov and Golding, 2-42).

The intellectual content and Marxist ideology in the Yiddish version were also downplayed, and the farcical elements emphasized. Critics found both the play and the performances lacking. Arthur Hornblow, writing for *Theatre Magazine*, criticized the non-Jewish Coburn, who played Hungershtolts, for lacking "all the Jewish mannerisms, his movement, voice and accent are all mechanical and superficial."[18] As for the play, he dismissed it as an "unconvincing *pot pourri* of melodrama, symbolism, musical comedy, burlesque and vaudeville" (Hornblow 31).

Following *Bronks Ekspres*, there were two other important Yiddish plays about labor, *Schmates (Rags)* and *Shop*, both by H. Leivick. A revolutionary who had escaped Siberia to come to America, Leivick supported himself as a paperhanger before earning fame for his poetry and plays. He is mostly remembered today as the author of *The Golem*, a blank-verse play about a 17th-century Jewish version of Frankenstein's monster.[19] But Leivick was also famous for his plays about the exploitation of Jewish immigrants on the Lower East Side.

Schmates (1921) centers on the character of Mordechai Maze, a worker in a rag factory. None of the men has energy to study the Bible any more: their knowledge of Jewish texts is fading. Whether they have abandoned Jewish tradition or it has abandoned them is difficult to say. The downtrodden workers are described at the beginning of Act III:

> There are about twenty men, all about fifty years of age. Several are already quite old. They work, but they aren't laborers. They lack the carriage, the awareness, or the assurance of a laborer. A kind of laziness, neglect, and scorn hangs over them all and in

---

[18] In later life, Coburn went on to a very successful film career, winning an Academy Award in 1943 for his role in *The More the Merrier*.
[19] Created to save Jews from Christian massacres.

the fingers of their hands, as they move among the dusty
rags, there is a sorrow and a helplessness…They look
like a flock of sheep that the storm has driven together
under one roof. There is a sense among the flock that
the storm will never end (Mlotek 35).

Maze's daughter becomes engaged to the son of the shop
owner. When the workers decide to organize for higher wages
and shorter working hours, they come to Maze to intervene with
his future son-in-law. He refuses to get involved; Maze is so
beaten down that he has no desire to better either his economic or
spiritual condition. Even at his daughter's engagement party, Maze
cannot cope; he rushes from the room in distress and refuses to
return despite his wife's pleas. He feels he has nothing to celebrate.

The immigrant men are also alienated from their sons. Calling
his boy Harry a "blood enemy," Maze complains: "He negates
me with one look, he destroys me…. As soon as he steps over the
threshold, it's as though he had brought the entire street in with
him and thrown it on me" (Mlotek 64). The son becomes, at least
in his father's eyes, a symbol of American society's rejection of
the poor and unwanted.

While Maze fantasizes about the day his family will shake
off the rags and dress up in their Sabbath finery, he understands
that his very soul has become tattered. "This is where everything
gets torn apart in me," he exclaims, pointing to his heart. "Into
pieces, tiny pieces. Torn, trampled…rags!…rags!…. Everyone,
everyone, stands and tears chunks, all, down to the last one!"
(Mlotek 60) Only in the shop is he able to externalize the rags
and take control over them. At the end of the play, Maze is on his
way back to the factory, the only place he feels at home.

Shop (1926), on the other hand, focuses on the character of
Wolf, a revolutionary turned sweatshop boss.[20] When the workers
go on strike, Wolf is caught between the interests of the scabs and
those of the strikers. To complicate matters, he is in love with
Mina, a striker and fellow revolutionary from the *Bund* (the Jewish

---

[20] Played by Jacob Ben-Ami, who had been Hungershtolts' son in the original cast of *Bronks Ekspres*.

labor organization) back in the Old Country. Mina disdains Wolf for selling out his ideals; instead she loves Lipman, a defeated and broken-down laborer similar to Maze in *Schmates*. Standing by his machine and staring into space, Lipman says: "It has to rip open, in the end. It has to, in the end. Who are we all? Sitting like dummies with our heads to the needles. All of us. And who is he, the so-called boss? A stammerer, a nothing" (Sandrow "Shop" 152-153).

The play ends with the announcement of Mina's and Lipman's engagement. But as the workers dance in celebration, the noise of the machines overtakes them. According to the stage directions: "The pattern of the dance is transformed into something which welds the people with the machines" (Sandrow "Shop" 183). At the height of this frenzy, a worker jumps from the roof to her death. The laborers have collectively lost their humanity; one has even lost her life. While this ending was likely influenced by the Italian Futurists, who were enraptured by technology to the point of romanticizing war, Leivick clearly sees machines not as objects of aesthetic appreciation but as malevolent forces that destroy human life. Capitalism has brought together the workers in solidarity, but it has also ultimately dehumanized them.

These same contradictions, inherent in transplanting the *shtetl* to the sweatshop, are brilliantly explored in the American-Yiddish film, *Uncle Moses* (1932). Starring Maurice Schwartz, the plot involves an immigrant garment-factory boss who views his workers as *mishpokhe* (family). When faced with a strike and the disdain of the woman he loves, the protagonist recognizes that money has corrupted all his relationships.

The Rise of the Broadway Jewish Drama

Despite Yiddish theater's avant-garde, creative energy, its audience was rapidly diminishing by the 1920s. According to a 1928 article in the *New York Evening Post*, "With the slowing up of immigration, the younger generation is drifting away from the language of its parents and prefers to go uptown to American shows for entertainment" ("In Praise" 30). Jewish audiences transferring their allegiance from the Yiddish theater to Broadway began a tradition of support for the mainstream performing arts in America that continues to this day.[21]

In the 1920s, much of the talent of the Yiddish stage – including writers, actors, directors and set designers – migrated to Broadway, where successful productions could earn huge profits. Significantly, a large portion of the theatrical producers were also Jewish; Jews dominated the "legitimate" stage as much they were beginning to dominate Hollywood. An article in *The American Hebrew* , the era's most widely read American-Jewish magazine, cited theatrical producers David Belasco, Lee Shubert and Sam Harris as living proof that Jews have "enacted an increasingly important role both in fostering the arts and in…creating art" (Carb 48).

The rise of Jewish theatrical producers was not only noted in Jewish publications. Thomas H. Dickinson observed in *The Nation* that the Jew demonstrated "just that combination of artistic discrimination and initiative in organization, that skill in fusing the diverse elements of an intimate and sensitive art with the touch-and-go, devil-may-care adventure of the curb market that is necessary in creating the modern dramatic production." Invoking familiar racial stereotypes, he concluded that the Jew possesses "that combination of qualities that make him the master of the tactics and strategy of the commercial theater" (689-690).

By the 1920s, Jewish audiences began to form an important segment of the New York market for theatrical productions.[22] Besides the Broadway production of *Bronks Ekspres*, there were many other plays about New York-Jewish life, some of which enjoyed mainstream popularity. For example, the non-Jewish playwright Anne Nichols scored the longest-running play of the decade with *Abie's Irish Rose* (1922), a comedy about a marriage between a Jewish boy and an Irish girl, neither of whom can bear to tell their immigrant fathers about the match. *Abie's Irish Rose*

---

[21] One of the reasons often cited nowadays for the decline of Broadway drama is the drop in Jewish patrons."Many of Broadway's problems are sociological, too large for the theater to confront as a business institution," writes Michael Goldstein. Among other things, he blames "the departure of thousands of suburban Jews, who have traditionally been among Broadway's biggest audience constituencies, for destinations Floridian…" (Goldstein 28).

[22] Reviewing *Two Blocks Away*, critic Percy Hammond of the *New York World* referred to the audience as "a large congregation" (Hammond 7).

spawned a host of imitators on both stage and screen, almost all of them by Jewish writers.

Set in an expensive apartment in the Bronx's Grand Concourse, *Abie's Irish Rose* shows what second-generation Jews aspired to in moving to the uptown and outer borough Jewish neighborhoods. (Merwin, "Performance of Jewish Ethnicity," 24). Leaving the Lower East Side often brought greater opportunities for economic and social advancement. Rather than ride the subway back to the factories on the Lower East Side, as Hungershtolts does in *Bronks Ekspres*, second-generation Jews were increasingly opening their own businesses; joining the construction trades; becoming teachers, social workers and pharmacists; taking government jobs; and even entering the professions.

Yet residential segregation actually increased during this outward migration of the 1920s. According to Deborah Dash Moore, Jews made up almost half the population in many Bronx and Brooklyn neighborhoods (Moore 21). Though they'd left the Lower East Side behind, second-generation New York Jews still lived in a world of their own. Finding a job was often based on ethnic contacts; Jews socialized almost exclusively with other Jews; shopped in the neighborhood;[23] and attended schools, synagogues, cinemas and theaters close by. The neighborhood "offered individual Jews an environment which mediated the stresses of acculturation. Just by going about his mundane activities in the neighborhood, a New York City Jew could feel equally American and Jewish – and unthreatened" (Moore 61).

However, based on a reading of the Jewish-themed plays of the decade, I believe as Jews moved into higher-status occupations, they experienced the conflict between Jewish and American values more acutely rather than less. To be sure, since Broadway plays were intended for a general audience, Jewish and other ethnic characters were often presented in highly stereotypical ways. The fathers in *Abie's Irish Rose*, for example, were straight out of vaudeville. Still the plays about second-generation Jewish life were filled, at root, with the same anxieties about the loss of

---

[23] Even kosher foods were readily available in the suburbs, although observance of dietary laws was declining rapidly in this period.

community that are evident in *Bronks Ekspres*.

Although most Jews no longer lived on the Lower East Side, the Jewish ghetto still functioned as an essential symbol of community. Moore writes: "The Lower East Side provided an emotional point of reference for both first- and second-generation Jews. It spawned, above all, the myth of the immigrant neighborhood as an organic community" (Moore 66).

The Lower East Side Reprised on Broadway

My historical review ends with a discussion of two Broadway plays encapsulating the tension between loyalty to the Lower East Side and the appeal of the suburbs. Aaron Hoffman's *Two Blocks Away*, which opened on Broadway, at the George M. Cohan Theatre on August 30, 1921, shows the negative consequences when a kindly shoemaker inherits a large sum of money and moves away from his Lower East Side neighborhood. Nate Pommerantz[24] had formerly given charity to all who needed it; in possession of a large inheritance, the shoemaker becomes mean and tight-fisted. Disdaining his former friends, Pommerantz moves to a palatial apartment in what the stage directions call an "aristocratic section" (probably Gramercy Park), and concentrates on accumulating more wealth. His addiction to prescription medicines is a sign that Pommerantz has lost both his bodily vigor and his self-control. Toward the end of the play, he smashes a mirror showing his now-intolerable reflection, thereby freeing himself from materialism. Only then can he resume his relationship with the beloved daughter he has alienated.

The mirror that reflects the character's moral infirmities – a device reminiscent, of course, of Oscar Wilde's novel, *The Picture of Dorian Gray* – is a metaphor for the stage itself, which reflects the largely Jewish theater audience's own desertion back at them. In a pivotal scene, Pommerantz's daughter, Jane, chooses the people of the Lower East Side over her stubborn father, who has

---

[24] Pommerantz was played by Barney Bernard, celebrated for his portrayals of Abe Potash in the long-running *Potash and Perlmutter* series about two hapless Jewish businessmen. *New York Times* reviewer Percy Hammond praised the actor's gift for "the comic observation, the obvious come-back, the frayed commonplace, and the humorous philosophy usual to his classic Potash role" (Hammond 7).

repudiated them. As she does so, the stage directions instruct the actor to face the audience – the only time this happens in the entire play. Jane vows she is "not going to lose them [her old friends], for money, or anything, or anybody" (Hoffman 82). Pommerantz's decision to move away from the immigrant neighborhood to satisfy his longings for upward social mobility is intended to register as a kind of betrayal of his people.

Pommerantz's old friends and neighbors might themselves be seen as grasping materialists, but the play does not criticize them for this; it only attacks Pommerantz's pretensions and self-delusions. The smashing of the mirror symbolizes the collapse of the shoemaker's inflated ego; paradoxically it also mends the ruptured relationship between Pommerantz and his community. By providing a neat climax to the play, it helped the audience *avoid* reflecting on how it might actually resemble the erring Pommerantz more than the redeemed Pommerantz.

At a time when Jews were rapidly acculturating into American society through their consumption of material goods, the idea of

Two Blocks Away. Stage Cast Shot.
Photographer: White Studio
Billy Rose Theatre Collection, The New York Public Library for the Performing Arts, Astor, Lenox and Tilden Foundations.

giving up physical comforts to re-identify with the ethnic group surely held limited appeal. On a conscious level, however, theater goers seemed to see the smashing of the mirror as both a vindication and a triumph. On the night of Hammond's August 1921 review, it actually halted the play. Upon smashing the mirror, Bernard "was urged ... to address the audience," which, according to the critic, "he did with becoming modesty and eloquence" (Hammond 7). The on-stage action was so powerful that it somehow seemed to necessitate the actor stepping out of his role and consolidating his bond with the audience.

Second-generation Jews were moving into the mainstream of American life to a much greater extent than their parents had been able to do. A final example, a comedy called *Poppa* (1928) by Bella and Samuel Spewack,[25] demonstrates this. Pincus Schwitzky is an immigrant insurance salesman seeking political office on the Lower East Side. He campaigns on a platform of providing modern conveniences – electric refrigerators, coin telephones (or "nickel slot machines") and garbage burners[26] – to each of the families in his district. The corrupt district leader Jake Harris appoints Schwitzky alderman, and promptly begins framing him on bribery charges. To turn the Bronx landlords against the new alderman, Harris warns that the new Frigidaires are so expensive that there is a "fat chance of landlords putting those things in" (Spewack and Spewack, 51) in the Bronx. The tenants will have to remain on the Lower East Side, in Pinky's district, if they want these modern conveniences. The usual pattern of Jews leaving the Lower East Side for a higher standard of living is being reversed; Pinky is removing the stigma of living in the ghetto.

After all, the Schwitzky family itself manages to be quite acculturated even while living on the Lower East Side. Act II takes place on Abraham Lincoln's Birthday; portraits of Lincoln and Washington hang on the walls, and the fire escapes are decorated with flags and bunting. The stage directions describe

---

[25] The successful husband-and-wife team later collaborated on musicals like *Boy Meets Girl* and *Kiss Me Kate*.

[26] These devices were already symbols of belonging to the middle class in the late 1920s, two decades before the gleaming (by then, suburban) kitchens of the post-World War II era.

an "atmosphere of sudden Second Avenue elegance." The acculturated appearance extends to the characters' dress. The father wears a "sort of shabby overcoat with collar turned up, a soft hat, pencils are stuck in his pockets, and he is carrying a much worn-out brief case, in which he carries his various insurance articles and applications" – the uniform of the average white-collar working man (Spewack and Spewack, 29). When he is appointed to political office, Schwitzky suddenly sports a "frock coat and silk hat" in addition to his overcoat, showing how much he has come up in the world. His wife boasts to the neighbors that "all day the people come to my husband for advice – like he was a dentist" (Spewack and Spewack, 66).

The family's pretensions to upward mobility are, however, difficult to sustain. When daughter Ruth becomes engaged to an uptown Jewish boy, his well-to-do mother is appalled by the shabbiness of the Schwitzkys' apartment and by the fact that the alderman earns no money. She worries her son will have to support the entire Schwitzky family, even though Ruth insists she will continue to work once married.

The plot against Schwitzky is ultimately frustrated through the use of technology, in this case a dictaphone that his ne'er-do-well son, Herbert, has ordered through the mail. The dictaphone records Harris threatening Schwitzky and engineering the frame-up.[27]

New York Times critic Brooks Atkinson, making an oblique reference to the large numbers of Jews in the audience, called the play "neither fish nor fowl nor good red herring." *Poppa*, he noted, "involves neighbors, local politics, family pride, a carpet sweeper and furniture on the installment plan – all to the sing-song animation of the Jewish-American accent. And whatever it may lack in originality it can readily supply through the sympathies of the authors and their audiences" (Atkinson 18).

---

[27] The resolution is reminiscent of Dion Boucicault's 1860 play *The Octoroon*, in which the identity of a murderer is discovered through the use of a photograph, at a time when cameras had just been invented. Ironically, the dictaphone in *Poppa* is viewed by the family as just a new household appliance, similar to the other labor-saving devices Pincus hopes to introduce on the Lower East Side.

Materialism vs. Jewish Identity

In the decades that followed, characters in Jewish-themed plays often wrestled with the costs of materialism in terms of undermining Jewish identity. From Clifford Odets' 1935 *Awake and Sing!* [28] to Neil Simon's comedies in the 1960s, and on through recent works by Jon Robin Baitz, Donald Margulies, Wendy Wasserstein and others, Jewish characters have attempted to reconcile Jewish values with the desire to be successful in American society.

Baitz's *The Substance of Fire* (1991) gives us Isaac Geldhart, founder of a New York publishing house noted for its obscure multi-volume works about the Holocaust. His grown children, who are part owners, try to persuade Geldhart to print books that will actually turn a profit, but the father is so obsessed with memorializing the Holocaust that he ultimately destroys both the business and his relationship with his children.

By contrast, Baitz's *Three Hotels* (1993) shows successful businessman Ken Hoyle wrestling with his betrayal of his own values. Hoyle (né Herskovitz) works for a company that markets baby formula to Third World countries with polluted water supplies. The play ends with him singing the Yiddish lullaby "Oyfn Pritpetchik" (By the Hearth) in an effort to reconnect with his childhood – and, by extension, his Jewish roots.

In Margulies' *The Loman Family Picnic* (1989),[29] a lower-middle-class Jewish family confronts the precariousness of its economic and spiritual survival. Set in Brooklyn during the mid-1960s, the drama centers around Herbie Loman demanding that his son Stewie hand over the gift money from his bar mitzvah. To avoid embarrassment, the Lomans have spent far more than they can afford on the affair. The spiritual meaning of the ceremony is entirely compromised in the name of keeping up appearances.

In Wasserstein's *The Sisters Rosensweig* (1993), three sisters find different paths to happiness: Gorgeous leads tours for the overdressed, fashion-conscious members of her Beth El

---

[28] Starring Yiddish stage veterans Morris Carnovsky and Stella Adler.
[29] A surrealistic take-off on the Arthur Miller classic, *Death of a Salesman*.

Sisterhood; Pfeni writes articles about the oppressed women of Afghanistan; and Sara – the most assimilated of the three – falls in love with an observant Jewish furrier who brings her to a grudging appreciation of her native culture.

Southern Jewish playwright Alfred Uhry examines some of the same issues with a lighter touch. In his best play, *Driving Miss Daisy* (1986), a fiercely independent, elderly widow in Atlanta finally admits that she is too old to drive. Her African-American chauffeur, Hoke, gradually becomes her closest friend. When Miss Daisy's synagogue is bombed during the civil rights movement, Hoke finds parallels to the lynchings of African-Americans under Jim Crow. There is little discussion of Miss Daisy's Jewishness in the play; it is left to the reader to infer how much her Jewishness plays a role in her friendship with Hoke.

Another prominent Jewish playwright, Herb Gardner, writes with great flair about Jewish men who conceal their spiritual emptiness behind an outward show of theatricality and verve. In *Conversations With My Father* (1994), Eddie[30] is the owner of a perpetually failing bar on Canal Street. Though he keeps renaming and redecorating it, Eddie never manages to fulfill his fantasy of moving the business uptown. The saloonkeeper has a very ambivalent view of his Jewish identity: he gets a tattoo specifically to be barred – under religious law banning disfigurement – from burial in a Jewish cemetery. When one of his few remaining patrons, a seemingly down-and-out former Yiddish actor, dies a millionaire, Eddie vents his frustration: "A millionaire, Charlie! Workin' in a loser language! He did everything wrong – and he was a hit…! The Big Bucks, why did they avoid me? Wherever I was, the bucks never came, and when I went to where the bucks are, they flew away like pigeons … like pigeons in the park" (Gardner 121).

Later Eddie recounts a recurrent dream: he is a new immigrant at Ellis Island, and the officials have refused him entrance to the country. "Old days," he explains, "you had a disease, they wouldn't let ya in. They mark on your coat with chalk, 'E' for

---

[30] Played on Broadway by Judd Hirsch.

eye, 'L' for lung, and they send ya back. In the dream, I got an 'H' for heart and they won't let me in...." (Gardner 121) Eddie's heart, Gardner seems to suggest, has atrophied in the course of his quest for material success; he has lost his capacity for empathy along with any positive feelings about his Jewishness.

While these examples take Jewish identity into account, few contemporary plays tackle the issues in a substantive way. Daniel Stern's comedy, *Barbra's Wedding* (2003) – about a Malibu interfaith couple living next door to Barbra Streisand on the day of her wedding to James Brolin – cashes in on Streisand's celebrity without saying anything new about Jews in Hollywood or the phenomenon of star-gazing. The husband, Jerry[31] has an air of stereotypical Jewish male fecklessness, but the only explicit reference to his Jewishness is a line about air-brushing the yarmulke from a photo of his meeting Robert Redford (at a Jewish affair), and a joke about no one at his wedding being able to pronounce the Hebrew blessings – including the rabbi. In my

Conversations With My Father. (L to R) Tony Gillan and Judd Hirsch.
Photographer: Marc Bryan-Brown
Presented by CTG / Ahmanson at the UCLA James A. Doolittle Theatre.

---

[31] Played in New York by John Pankow.

review for the *New York Jewish Week*, I conclude that "the lackluster *Barbra's Wedding* sells out to the same fickle, materialistic gods that watch over its chronically dissatisfied, simplistically written characters. Is the title false advertising? You decide." (Merwin, "Trouble," 43)

Also Hollywood-themed but not much better in terms of analyzing its main character's Jewishness, is Marsha Lebby and John Lollos' *Mr. Goldwyn* (2002). The biographical play[32] focuses on the narcissistic businessman who pulled himself up by his immigrant bootstraps to become one of the most successful movie producers in history. But Goldwyn's psychology remains largely unexplored, including his intensely ambivalent feelings about being Jewish.

Indeed, many celebrated plays by Jewish playwrights do not have strong Jewish themes. Possibly the most important play of the 1990s, Tony Kushner's *Angels in America* (1992), has a compelling Jewish character at its center: Roy Cohn, the crooked lawyer who was Sen. Joseph McCarthy's right hand. But Kushner is much more concerned with dramatizing Roy's homosexual identity than his Jewish identity. Similarly, the 2003 Tony Award for Best Play went to Richard Greenberg's *Take Me Out*, a play about a gay baseball star whose public announcement of his homosexuality leads to murder when teammates and friends cannot contain their homophobia.

Ironically *Back Stage*, the New York newspaper of the performing arts, recently identified a new "gay sensibility" in contemporary culture that often centers on issues of assimilation. Has the "Jewish sensibility" so prevalent in early 20th-century theater morphed into a gay sensibility? Jeff Marx, quoted in the *Back Stage* article, said, "In the future, all American culture will be gay-themed" (Haagensen 27). Perhaps American culture has already become Jewish-themed to such an extent that even Jewish playwrights (many of whom are gay) find more dramatic potential in a part of their identities that is still marginalized and discriminated against.

---

[32] Starring Alan King in New York.

As the boundaries between Jewish life and American society continue to shift, it becomes increasingly difficult to separate "Jewish" values from American ones. Perhaps the meaning of Jewishness needs to be redefined in every generation, or at different times throughout each individual's life. American Jews will no doubt continue to struggle with the challenges of maintaining their ethnic distinctiveness and of deciding how to carve out a space for the expression of their Jewish sensibility. But this will take place in a society that, however much it celebrates ethnic diversity, is impatient with those who, like Jews, insist on the perpetuation of a particular ethnic identity. If the melting pot ultimately makes other hyphnated Americans feel disconnected from a sense of heritage and tradition that gives meaning and purpose to their lives, Jews may yet have another lesson to teach America.

Works Cited

Atkinson, J. Brooks. Rev. of *Poppa*. *New York Times*. 25 December 1928: 18.

Baitz, Jon Robin. *The Substance of Fire and Other Plays*. New York: Theatre Communications Group, 1993.

Baitz, Jon Robin. *Three Hotels: Plays and Monologues*. New York: Theatre Communications Group, 1994.

Berkowitz, Joel. *Shakespeare on the American Yiddish Stage*. Iowa City: University of Iowa Press, 2002.

Bronner, Simon. "Reading Consumer Culture." in Bronner, ed., *Consuming Visions: Accumulation and Display of Goods in America, 1880-1920*. New York: W.W. Norton & Company, 1989.

Buckley, Christopher. *Washington Schlepped Here: Walking in the Nation's Capital*. New York: Crown Publishers, 2003.

Cahan, Abraham. "A Nayer Sort Comedia Af Der Yiddisher Biene." ("A New Kind of Comedy on the Yiddish Stage.") *Forvertz* (*Forward*). 5 January 1919: 5.

Carb, David. "A Major Impetus in the American Theatre: The Jew Is Enacting Increasingly Important Role as Creator and Sponsor of Our Native Drama." *American Hebrew*. 22 November 1929: 48.

Dickinson, Thomas H. "The Jew in the Theater." *The Nation*. 13 June 1923: 689-90.

Dymov, Osip. *Bronx Express*. In Sandrow, trans., *God, Man and Devil*.

Ervine, St. John. Rev. of *Poppa*. *New York Morning World*. 26 December 1928: 19.

Fox, Stephen. *The Mirror Makers: A History of American Advertising and Its Creators*. New York: William Morrow & Company, 1984.

Gardner, Herb. *Conversations With My Father*. New York: Doubleday Books, 1994.

Golding, Samuel. *Bronx Express*. Unpublished typescript in New York Public Library, Billy Rose Theatre Collection.

Goldstein, Michael. "Reinventing Broadway." *New York Magazine*. 29 May 1995: 28-32.

Hammond, Percy. Rev. of *Partners Again*. *New York Tribune*. 31 August 1921.

Heinze, Andrew R. *Adapting to Abundance: Jewish Immigrants, Mass Consumption, and the Search for American Identity*. New York, Columbia University Press, 1990.

Heinze, Andrew R. "Jewish Women and the Making of an American Home," In Jennifer Scanlon, ed., *The Gender and Consumer Culture Reader*. New York: New York University Press, 2000.

Hoffman, Aaron. *Two Blocks Away*. New York: Samuel French, 1925.

Hornblow, Arthur. Rev. of *Bronx Express*. *Theatre Magazine* . July 1922: 31.

"In Praise of Muni Wisenfrend." *New York Evening Post*. 21 January 1928: 30.

Joselit, Jenna Weissman. *The Wonders of America: Reinventing Jewish Culture, 1880-1950*. New York: Hill & Wang, 1994.

Kushner, Tony. *Angels in America: Millennium Approaches*. New York: Theater Communications Group, 1992.

Leach, William. *Land of Desire: Merchants, Power and the Rise of a New American Culture*. New York: Pantheon Books, 1993.

Leivick, H. *Schmates* (unpub. trans. by Chana Mlotek for the Folksbiene Yiddish Theatre of New York.)

Lifson, David S. *The Yiddish Theatre in America*. New York: Thomas Yoseloff, 1965.

Margulies, Donald. *The Loman Family Picnic*. New York: Dramatists Play Service, 1994.

Merwin, Ted. "The Performance of Jewish Ethnicity in Anne Nichols' *Abie's Irish Rose*," Journal of American Ethnic History 20:2 (Winter 2001), 3-37.

——. "Trouble in Paradise." (Rev. of *Barbra's Wedding*.) *New York Jewish Week*. 21 March 2003: 43.

Moore, Deborah Dash. *At Home in America: Second Generation New York Jews,* New York: Columbia University Press, 1981.

Norris, James D. *Advertising and the Transformation of American Society, 1865-1920*. New York: Greenwood Press, 1990.

O'Neill, Eugene. *The Hairy Ape*. London: Jonathan Cape, 1923.

Rich, Frank (with Lisa Aronson). *The Theatre Art of Boris Aronson*. New York: Alfred A. Knopf, 1987.

Rice, Elmer. *The Adding Machine*. New York: Samuel French, 1929.

Rice, Elmer. *The Subway*. New York: Samuel French, 1929.

Sandrow, Nahma. *God, Man and Devil: Yiddish Plays in Translation*. Syracuse, NY: Syracuse University Press, 1999.

Sandrow, Nahma. *Vagabond Stars: A World History of Yiddish Theatre*. Syracuse, NY: Syracuse University Press, 1977.

Spewack, Bella and Samuel. *Poppa*. New York: Samuel French, 1928.

Uhry, Alfred. *Driving Miss Daisy*. New York: Theatre Communications Group, 1988.

Wasserstein, Wendy. *The Sisters Rosensweig*. New York: Harcourt Trade Publishers, 1993.

Zangwill, Israel. *The Melting Pot*. New York: Macmillan, 1909.

Chapter Three

IMAGE:
Jewish Humor in Our Popular Culture: The Little Men Come and Go

By Adam Rovner

"Comedy is [. . .] the dessert, a bit like meringue." – *Woody Allen*

"Chocolate is Jewish and fudge is goyish." – *Lenny Bruce*

I f comedy is dessert, what sort of confection is Jewish comedy? Would Lenny Bruce consider meringue Jewish? Perhaps pies – Jewish or not – are only like comedy when they are thrown in someone's face. When a well-aimed pie hits its mark, the target's face is obscured. Comedy often entails such a doubly-directed distortion: the faces of both the laughing joker and his straight man undergo change. This essay explores how the image of the Jew as comic butt *and* comic wit has been represented or misrepresented in American popular culture

It is difficult to answer the deceptively simple question, "What is Jewish humor?" *"And who wants to know?"* is probably the most identifiably Jewish retort and, in some ways, also the last word on the subject. Secondary scholarly literature, not to mention the folk wisdom of everyday conversation, often refers to something called "Jewish humor" without bothering to offer a serious description. Like the "I-know-it-when-I-see-it" definition of obscenity, the essence of Jewish humor remains elusive.

This essay considers in detail two works by Jewish writers that are often deemed obscene: Philip Roth's 1969 novel *Portnoy's Complaint,* and Adam Herz's screenplay for the 1999 film *American Pie.* Scenes linking orality with sexuality in both the novel and the film serve as metaphors for the evolution of American-Jewish humor over the last three decades, a period that parallels the unprecedented acceptance of Jews and Jewish life into the American cultural and socio-political mainstream. Comparative treatment of these works exposes a changing dynamic of American-Jewish identity and comic self-image. The very notion of a distinctive Jewish humor is intimately connected to the image of the Jew in American popular culture. It also reflects the prevailing belief in fundamental Jewish difference – a belief that pop culture trends may now be nibbling away at.

One problem with the concept of Jewish humor is that the phrase simply isn't meaningful in any critical sense. There are as many *kinds* of Jewish humor as there are kinds of Jews. For example, the Jewish-mother cliché of American jokes doesn't make sense in Hebrew jokes – because the basic assumption is that most Israelis *have* a Jewish mother. So the overbearing parent figure, in Israeli humor, becomes a Polish mother. Humor is culturally determined. To "get" the joke or comic sketch, the audience must share some basic cultural knowledge with the narrator. The analysis that follows aims to present a working understanding of what characterizes Jewish humor in America – where most Jews are descendents of Ashkenazi immigrants arriving in the United States in the early 20th century.

Some thoughtful analysts have attempted to record their recipes for Jewish humor. Writing in 1951, Irving Howe thought "self-criticism" verging on "self-denunciation" leavened Jewish humor (Howe 212). Literary scholar Robert Alter suggested that Jewish humor is sweetened with wry and homey ingredients (Alter 255). Critic David Roskies characterized Jewish humor as spiced with paradox and incongruity (Roskies 64-70). Israeli humor theorist and psychologist Avner Ziv cooked up this suspiciously tautological formula: "Jewish humor is humor created by Jews, reflecting special aspects of Jewish life" (Ziv 145). While helpful in some respects, Ziv's definition is too broad to effectively get at the specific characteristics of Jewish humor in America.

Academics are not the only ones hard-pressed to define Jewish humor. Professional comedians have offered their own theories. Comedian Shelly Berman believed that Jewish humor was fundamentally tied to suffering (Nachman 301), while Mel Brooks had the *chutzpah* to deny the very existence of Jewish humor (qtd. Rosenblatt). Other critics, writers and comedians have offered differing interpretations,[1] but all of these piquant descriptions leave one hungry for something more substantial.

The Rise of the " Little Man"

In the quest to define Jewish humor, it is worthwhile to survey the development of the concept, which has changed greatly in the last 150 years. Our contemporary understanding of Jewish humor seems to derive from the concept of *Judenwitz*[2], an acerbic kind of wit most often associated with Heinrich Heine. Having converted to Christianity for personal advancement, the great German poet and wit straddled two cultures. But his sympathies remained with the Jewish "little man." Heine introduced several Yiddishisms into the German language and injected an appreciation of Jewish folkways into the literary canon.[3]

In his recent book, *Inciting Laughter*, scholar Jefferson Chase argues that *Judenwitz* came to be viewed over time as a malicious

---

[1] See essays by Berger and Whitfield for their views on Jewish humor. Berger in particular focuses on comedians' and actors' views on Jewish humor.

[2] In German, literally, "Jewish humor."

[3] Several of Heine's references to Judaism revolve around food. In "A Winter's Tale" (1844), he depicts a Jewish mother eager to cook for her returning son. In Heine's *The Rabbi of Bacherach* (1840), a Jewish knight returns home only to eat. And in *The Princess Sabbath* (1850), Heine refers to challah, cholent and other Jewish fare.

and debased form of humor foreign to German national identity (Chase 2). By the mid 1800s Jews had entered the mainstream of German culture so completely that they were no longer easily distinguishable from gentiles. Those opposed to Jewish inclusion sought a marker of ethnic distinctiveness: they identified it in the stylistic elements of several Jewish writers. These elements came to be sneeringly referred to as *Judenwitz*. Heine's deriders and imitators, alike, utilized the conventions of a supposed Jewish dialect in their *feuilletons* to endow the written word with the aroma of garlic commonly believed to typify the ghetto Jew.

Chase concludes that *Judenwitz* became "a pejorative concept that marginalized a perceived form of minority speech and helped to redefine the identity of the self-appointed mainstream" (Chase 3). If Chase's theory is correct, then the conception of a particular Jewish humor was originally tied to 19th-century German anti-Semitism – itself a reaction to burgeoning Jewish emancipation. In 1944, political philosopher Hannah Arendt pointed out that Heine felt himself in allegiance with the *schlemiels*[4] of the world – those innocent, downtrodden, "pariah" people who figured in many of his poems, often explicitly as Jews (75). She believed that Heine, Franz Kafka and Charlie Chaplin all utilized the comic persona of the "little man" to describe the situation of the Jew in the modern world.[5]

Many believe that Jewish humor transforms a long history of painful experience into laughter, but several notable thinkers have argued just the opposite: that Jewish humor turns laughter into pain. Sigmund Freud famously voiced the opinion that Jewish humor is essentially self-deprecating. In his *Jokes and Their Relations to the Unconscious* (1905), Freud offered the following observation: "I do not know whether there are many other instances of a people making fun to such a degree of its own character" (113). Psychoanalyst Theodor Reik, following Freud, found in the masochism of this supposed self-mockery evidence of a particular Jewish psychopathology.[6] More modern accounts

---

[4]   In Yiddish, "a blunderer." See in particular Part IV of *The Princess Sabbath*, wherein Heine calls himself a descendant of the biblical Shelumiel (Num.l.6), said to have met with an unhappy end.
[5]   See also Yates for his influential treatment of the "little man" in American literature, particularly his Jewish incarnation (331-350).
[6]   See Grotjahn for a strong version of the Jewish-humor-as-masochism thesis.

have continued to associate supposed Jewish qualities with psychological dysfunction. A study published in 1981 traced the etiology of professional comedians to the childhood onset of a series of "presenting symptoms," grouped under the heading: "The Child Schlemiel" (Fisher and Fisher 109-131).[7]

The self-deprecation thesis may be traced back to pseudo-scientific racial theories popular in Germany during the late 19th and early 20th centuries. Sander Gilman has exposed how various negative assessments of Jewish distinctiveness helped cement the concept of self-hatred – a concept springing, at least in part, from 19th century notions of Jewish humor. When Freud began to formulate his views on wit, Jewish humor was associated with popular published editions of dirty jokes (Gilman 266). At the time, Jews were thought to succumb to sexual depravity and mental infirmity in greater numbers than non-Jews. The identification of this supposed propensity toward illness was an attempt by anti-Semitic elements to reify Jewish difference. Jewish moral and mental decline was alternately blamed on several factors, including: sexual over stimulation (thought by some to be triggered by the spices of traditional Jewish food), faulty reasoning (epitomized by Talmudic learning and its strategies for aggressively playful questioning, particularly the back-and-forth practice of *pilpul*[8]), and even the cultural process of assimilation itself.[9]

The Freudian view that self-castigation typifies Jewish humor still seems to prevail today, nearly 100 years after the publication of *Jokes and Their Relation to the Unconscious*. The once-prevalent undertone of anti-Semitism that validated Freud's theories is no longer obvious in America, though accusations of self-hatred are apt to dog professional humorists. American Jewish comedians have long struggled to define the line between laughing *with* and laughing *at* Jewish stereotypes. Some – like Fanny Brice, Milton Berle and Sam Levenson – rejected outright jokes about,

---

[7] The study focused on both Jewish and non-Jewish comedians.
[8] From Hebrew, "to debate hotly." Through *pilpul*, yeshiva students were expected to view a problem from all angles. The study technique clearly promoted a taste for the antithetical logic and rational absurdities that characterize the well-known folk tales of the Wise Men of Chelm and Hershele Ostropoler.
[9] See Gilman, esp. Chapter 5.

as Levenson put it, the "little Jew" (qtd. in Popkin 50). In contemporary culture, Woody Allen and Philip Roth have been accused of self-hatred and have playfully responded to such criticisms in their work. Given the historical interconnectedness of Jewish humor, anti-Semitism and the notion of self-hatred, it is not surprising that the popularity of Woody Allen's and Philip Roth's unmistakably Jewish and overtly Freudian humor has reinforced the association of Jews and self-deprecation in popular consciousness.[10]

However, humor scholarship has begun to assail the widespread belief, pioneered by Freud, that self-mockery characterizes Jewish humor. In his article "Exploring the Thesis of the Self-Deprecating Jewish Sense of Humor," scholar Christie Davies argues that the self-deprecation thesis confuses the generic conventions of humor with malicious stereotypes (192-193). "Jewish humor," he writes, "is a special case of a more general phenomenon, namely, the asymmetry between the humor of culturally dominant majorities and the humor of culturally subordinate minority groups" (189-190). In other words, marginal groups adopt self-deprecation as a defense strategy; Jews are particularly adept at transforming this defense mechanism into successful comedy.

Folklorist Dan Ben-Amos also casts doubt on the validity of the self-mockery thesis. In 1973, he found evidence not of masochism but, rather, of a kind of sadism (130). Humor, he wrote, can function "as a vehicle of verbal aggression toward those from whom the narrator distinguishes himself unequivocally" (Ben-Amos 123). In other words, a secular-Jewish academic recounting a joke about a Hassidic *mohel*[11] is not demonstrating self-hatred or masochism: he is merely distinguishing himself from the values and world view of the Hassids. The joke-teller's humor, then, combines elements of aggression and feelings of superiority.

---

[10] Since 1981, the still-popular *Big Book of Jewish Humor*, edited by William Novak and Moshe Waldoks, has prepared a new generation of Jews to embrace the idea of their own comic psychopathology. The editors note that psychiatrist jokes have supplanted rabbi jokes in much of Jewish joke-telling (48).

[11] In Hebrew, "circumciser."

    The positive connotation many of us attach to Jewish humor
is recent, as is the notion that Jews even *have* a sense of humor.
Until roughly 100 years ago, they were considered sober and
humor*less,* according to Ben-Amos (113).[12] Other contemporary
scholars insist upon an ancient tradition of Jewish humor – finding
wordplay, irony and sarcasm in religious texts.[13] Writing in British
mandatory Palestine in 1934, Zionist leader and cultural critic
Nahum Sokolov associated Jewish humor with a genius for irony.
He traced the origins of Jewish humor to the practice of *pilpul*
(423).[14] Whatever the merits of the claims for a religiously
grounded tradition of humor, Jews as an ethnic group have come
to be identified with humor in America.

Kaddish for the Little Man: The 1950s

Jewish humor has been a topic of periodic eulogizing in the United
States at least since the 1950s. In the aftermath of the Holocaust,
influential American-Jewish intellectuals paid a curious amount
of attention to the genre. In retrospect, it seems unlikely that the
threat of extinction would prompt concern for the future of
comedy. However, proof of Jewish vulnerability and the
industrialized world's ambivalence to mass atrocity turned many
American-Jewish thinkers toward questions of cultural continuity.
Critics often have characterized Jewish humor as "laughter
through tears." Such a conceptualization apparently derives from
Sholem Aleichem's description of his own comic imperative: "Not
to cry out of spite! Only to laugh out of spite, *only to laugh*" (qtd.
in Madison 96). One would expect, then, that Jewish humor would
survive the Holocaust, if only for spite. Indeed its victims turned
to humor, frequently gallows humor, throughout the war; and its
survivors, to playful refigurations of the catastrophe after
liberation.[15]
    Yet leading critics on both the right and the left explicitly

---

[12] See also Ziv 145.
[13] *Humor,* the scholarly journal of the International Society for Humor Studies, hosts an ongoing
debate on whether the Old Testament possesses comic elements. For examples, see
Friedman, Morreall.
[14] See note 6. Also see Stora-Sandor for a similar point.
[15] See Lipman's excellent study of humor in the Holocaust.

linked the Holocaust to Jewish humor. Irving Kristol mourned the passing of Jewish humor in his 1951 essay, "Is Jewish Humor Dead? The Rise and Fall of the Jewish Joke." He argued that "what we call Jewish humor is Yiddish humor" (433), and that it had "died with its humorists when the Nazis killed off the Jews of Eastern Europe" (431). In another essay from 1951, "The Nature of Jewish Laughter," Irving Howe denied the very existence of Jewish humor – claiming it "is not humorous [but] disturbing and upsetting, its phrases dipped in tragedy" (214). For Howe, a strong proponent of Yiddish culture, the important literary achievements of Jewish comic writers "came to an end in Hitler's slaughterhouses" (211). Both he and Kristol linked Jewish humor to a tradition of Yiddish folklore and the literature of classical-era writers, specifically Sholem Aleichem, who had detailed in story after story the dignity of the common man through *schlemiel* figures. He established, or at least entrenched, the trope of the comic endurance of the *kleyne mentshelekh*.[16]

Critic Henry Popkin added his voice to the chorus of concern in an article published in 1952, "The Vanishing Jew of Our Popular Culture: The Little Man Who Is No Longer There." His content analysis of comic strips, novels, theater productions, film, television, radio and stand-up comedy routines led to the alarming conclusion that Jewish characters, themes and humor had all but disappeared from the realm of American popular entertainment. Popkin attributed the decline of a Jewish media presence to Hitler (46). Rather than concede that the Final Solution had depleted the sources of Jewish creativity, as Kristol and Howe had done, Popkin believed that the specter of anti-Semitism prompted those in the culture industry to consider Jews an unsuitable comic subject. He angrily charged that "the American answer to the banishment of the Jews from public life in Germany was the banishment of Jewish figures from the popular arts – in the United States" (46).

For Popkin, American popular culture in the 1940s and '50s witnessed the emergence of a taboo grounded in "misguided

---

16 In Yiddish, "little men."

benevolence" – the mistaken belief that concealment of Jewish specificity would lead to a decrease in anti-Semitism. The many examples Popkin cites of "de-Semitized" popular culture suggests that some form of suppression of Jewish identity was indeed at work in that era. However, his discovery of "an unwritten law that makes the Jew the little man who isn't there" is surely an overstatement (46). Consider the immensely popular radio situation comedy *The Goldbergs*, broadcast between 1929 and 1950. In 1949, the television incarnation of *The Goldbergs* ranked second in ratings only to the variety show hosted by Milton Berle (Romeyn and Kugelmass 53). The Jewish "Mr. Television" was a towering entertainment presence in the postwar period. He often worked Yiddish expressions and an urban, Jewish sensibility into his act. His exuberant stage persona and personal identification as a Jew[17] defined Uncle Miltie as anything but an "absent Jewish little man."

Popkin marshals the most persuasive evidence of the vanishing Jew in his discussion of Hollywood films; from the mid 1930s to the '50s, the studios clearly were reluctant to tackle Jewish themes and characters. Attributing this "de-Semitization" to timidity or fear of anti-Semitic backlash is not the whole story, though. The tendency to conceal Jewish particularity argues equally strongly for a strident desire among Jews to fully assimilate into a wartime and postwar American society struggling with integrationist values. Many World War II veterans returning to college or to the workforce were willing to tolerate diversity in civilian life – so long as the facts of difference could be overlooked.

Another possible explanation of this de-Semitization harkens back to 1934, when imposition of the notorious Hays Code prohibited Hollywood from ridiculing or negatively depicting religious groups. Anxious not to tangle with the code's enforcers, filmmakers removed any elements pointing to Jewish particularity – most notably, dialect. Nor can one discount economic rationales for the vanishing Jew. A desire to reach the largest possible audience, without fear of alienating people unfamiliar with Jewish

---

[17] Berle physically attacked a headline comedian who demeaned him as a Jew in 1925 and sent him to the hospital. He also refused to do stereotypical Jewish characters familiar to him from his vaudeville roots (Epstein *The Haunted Smile* 49, 134).

characters and Judaism, likely contributed to de-Semitization.

In 1958, several years after Popkin had first highlighted the so-called Jewish disappearance, Bernard Rosenberg and Gilbert Shapiro described the Jewish propensity toward humor as a response to cultural marginality. The assimilation of American Jews into mainstream culture, which had once seemed inevitable, was interrupted and perhaps forever forestalled by the Holocaust (Rosenberg and Shapiro 80). The catastrophe that befell European Jewry, the sociologists implied, had triggered an anti-assimilationist response among American Jews. In their view, Hitler's genocide may have *ensured* rather than threatened the survival of the Jewish joke.

The Americanization of the Little Man: 1960s to the Present

In the decade following the predictions of Jewish humor's imminent death, author Wallace Markfield proposed an intriguing and more optimistic prognosis. He argued that American humor was so Yiddishized that it had in fact become indistinguishable from Jewish humor (Markfield 114-115).[18] Sydney Lumet turned Markfield's novel, *To an Early Grave*, into the 1968 movie *Bye, Bye Braverman*. The film portrayed a variety of Jewish little men – middle age, middle-class *schlemiels* winding their circuitous way to a friend's funeral.[19] As if to prove Markfield's point, screenwriter Herb Sargent did not downplay the film characters' Jewishness, perhaps concluding that an American public familiar with Yiddishisms from Madison Avenue would not reject his script.

The 1960s saw not the de-Semitization but the increasing Yiddishization of American humor. Comic insider Albert Goldman even claimed Jewish humor hadn't existed in the American media before the 1950s ("Laughtermakers" 80).[20] As the '60s turned to the '70s, Jewish authors greater in stature than

---

[18] See also Goldman (1971) 170.
[19] Interestingly, both versions include a character who is a thinly-veiled Irving Howe and center around the death of a character recalling author and critic Isaac Rosenfeld.
[20] See also Cohen's claim that Jewish humor "openly flourished" in America only since the 1950s (172).

Markfield began to dominate American arts and letters – writers like Bernard Malamud and future Nobel laureates Saul Bellow (1976) and I.B. Singer (1978).

Literary scholar Ruth Wisse, in her seminal work *The Schlemiel as Modern Hero*, suggested that the black comedy and gallows humor so popular in postwar American writing had Yiddish roots (48). Several masters of dark comic fiction of the 1950s, '60s and '70s were Jewish Americans – including Max Apple, Bruce Jay Friedman, Joseph Heller and notably Philip Roth, whom Wisse treats in her book. Together they established the cynical, maladjusted, comic "little man" as the most significant image of the Jew in American popular consciousness.[21]

In contemporary American society, the identification of Jews with humor carries few negative connotations. The connection between Jews and humor has been so powerful that a 1980 study by psychologist Samuel Janus found that although Jews comprised only 3% of the population, 80% of professional comics identified themselves as Jewish (259). This imbalance has likely diminished as other minority groups ascended the stand-up comedy stage in the last two decades. But as stereotypes go, Jews being funny is not so bad. The association has even taken on the gloss of a modern theory of Jewish election – Jews are the people chosen to be funny. Lawrence Epstein has gone so far as to suggest humor is a substitute religion for American Jews (*The Haunted Smile* 292). Jews might now be considered the people of the *joke* book.[22]

Toward a New Definition of Jewish Humor

According to Christie Davies's content analysis of Jewish jokes, there are "*far* more Jewish jokes about the perils and temptations of assimilation, or apostasy, about rule and boundary breaking and about imitation of and masquerading as members of another group" than with any other ethnic group ("An Explanation of Jewish Jokes" 368).[23] Diaspora Jewry's fascination with integration and with seeing Judaism reflected in the character of

---

[21] Compare to Sig Altman's similar claims.
[22] Cf. Oring's "The People of the Joke."
[23] See also Davies (1991) 204ff1; and Dundes 197-198.

the non-Jew, and vice versa, is instructive. I offer the following definition: Jewish humor is primarily humor about the threat or fear of *no longer* being identifiably Jewish. Jewish humor – specifically its American variant – is recognizable precisely because it is poised between inclusion and exclusion and deals with the perils to identity posed by widespread cultural acceptance. Jewish humor may be a last-ditch means to assert cultural difference in the face of overwhelming acceptance. Even more radically, Jewish humor may represent a means for *maintaining* cultural difference.

Wisse noted that despite his bumbling ways, rotten luck and frequent persecution, the *schlemiel* of classical-era Yiddish literature managed to endure with his Jewish sensibility and identity intact. The little man, she concludes, "represents the triumph of identity despite the failure of circumstance" (53). Wisse seems to have meant that a richness and integrity of Jewish character compensated for the material poverty and imminent dangers faced by the *kleyne mentshelekh* in Yiddish literature. Jewish humor in America subverts Wisse's paradigm and yields the punch line to my thesis: The characters in American-Jewish humor represent the *failure* of identity due to the *triumph* of circumstance.

Thanks to the successes of Jewish assimilation and the increasing wealth, artistic influence and political power of American Jewry, the widespread insistence on Jewish difference has mostly disappeared from popular culture. But humor is an area where Jewish peculiarity is still conspicuous. I believe this persistent distinctiveness may derive more from Jewish desires for exclusivity than from the ambivalence of the non-Jewish majority.

Traditional Jewish belief in election is grounded in a sense of a unique mission, divinely revealed by God in sacred texts. At the same time, circumstances have mocked Jewish election; the incongruity between aspiration and reality may be the wellspring for a great deal of Jewish humor.[24] Much of diasporic history

---

[24] Roskies attributes Jewish humor to a disconnect between the worldly reality of Jews in Eastern Europe and what those Jews believed should be their lot according to God's promises (esp. 64-70). Humor theorists tend to support the view that incongruity is a necessary cause for humor. The paradox of Jewish reality in persecuted countries compared to beliefs in election would, then, logically provide a breeding ground for a comic sense of cosmic incongruity.

presents Jews as a people abandoned by God. Hostile dominant cultures depicted the Jew as selfish, evil and ungrateful. But in Jewish folklore, classical-era Yiddish literature and modern fiction and film, the Jew is frequently a harmless, innocent incompetent. The folkways of the common man so valued by Heine, the dignity of the suffering *kleyne mentshelekh* of Sholem Aleichem, the harried innocence of Charlie Chaplin's Little Tramp as he impersonates the Great Dictator – all converge in the American fascination with the plight of the little man, as represented by the enduring and endearing figure of the *schlemiel*.

Playing with Food: The Little Man's Hungry Heart

If food is to Jewish humor what drink is to Irish humor, as critic Mark Shechner suggested in 1974 (416), then it is valuable to look at how representations of food have changed in Jewish comic works. What does this change say about the future of American-Jewish humor? And more broadly, what does it tell us about cultural identity and the image of Jews in American society?

Food preference is an important element in defining Jewish identity. In his psychoanalytic study of Jewish wit, Theodor Reik observed in 1962 that "food preferences remind us of common meals in which certain dishes and combinations of them were preferred. In a similar way, people [are] reminded of their original totemistic meals in which the tribes established and renewed their community" (141). The laws of *kashrut*[25] remain defining elements in Jewish communal and family life. And the two most widely observed Jewish holidays in contemporary America, Passover and Yom Kippur, center around dietary rituals: the *seder* and the fast.

In everyday practice, food preferences may be one of the few identifiable markers of ethnic or religious identity.[26] Since much of humor in general is about rule-breaking,[27] and since Judaism has strict rules on clean and unclean foods and proper dietary ritual, we can expect that much humor created by Jews would

---

[25] In Hebrew, the "fitness or legitimacy" of food.
[26] For an entertaining account of how food taboos regulate Jewish sexual conduct see Rosenfeld.
[27] See Bakhtin 10; and Saroglou 203.

deal with transgressing, or anxiety about transgressing, these rules. It is no surprise, then, that so many Jewish jokes have to do with food.[28]

Now that the table has been set, so to speak, I can explore the trajectory of Jewish comic expression since the publication of *Portnoy's Complaint*. Philip Roth's best-known novel – featuring perhaps the most notorious figure of an overbearing and food-obsessed Jewish mother in American literature – was heralded by both accolades and attacks when it appeared. At the center of the hand-wringing was a concern that the novel would embarrass or defame Judaism because of explicit descriptions of masturbation, sexual exploits and a burlesque depiction of Jewish family life. Critical reaction was split. Some saw the novel as vulgar or self-hating, others as liberating or affirming. Readers were less ambivalent. They made it a No. 1 best-seller and pop culture phenomenon – "the most talked-about novel of our time," as the cover notes put it. In his wide-ranging study, *The Comic Image of the Jew*, critic Sig Altman notes that by 1969 readers were already "conditioned to laugh at the American Jew" (112). *Portnoy's Complaint* is the perfect example, for Altman, of a pop-culture artifact that helped to enshrine the image of the Jew as a self-deprecatory *schlemiel*. Not surprisingly, this essentializing vision of Jews and Jewish humor was intimately connected in the novel to an overtly Freudian narrative.

Portnoy's Complaint is a *tour de force* performance that relies on the impeccable timing, Yiddish word play and exploitation of interpersonal tensions associated with many of the great Jewish comedians. The narrative takes the form of a monologue – presented by the protagonist, Alexander Portnoy – to his analyst, Dr. Spielvogel. Portnoy (possibly an anagram of "porn-toy") seeks treatment for impotence, triggered by a sense of shame and dread rooted in his relationship with his mother. Dr. Spielvogel describes Portnoy's complaint as if the malady were an entry in the standard *Diagnostic and Statistical Manual of Mental Disorders*: a morbid

---

[28] The plethora of Jewish waiter jokes, jokes about rabbis eating pork, about Jews loving Chinese food, about Jewish mothers foisting heaping plates on their children, are the most ready examples.

tendency toward "auto-eroticism and oral coitus" (epigraph).

Schechner heralded the novel as a "spectacular attempt at Freudian fiction" (414). *Portnoy's Complaint* is deeply influenced by Freudian thinking and the psychoanalytic method. Roth makes explicit reference to Freud's "The Most Prevalent Form of Degradation in Erotic Life," and even titles a section of the book after the famous 1912 essay. When the *New American Review* excerpted Roth's forthcoming novel in 1968, it was titled "Civilization and Its Discontents" – clearly an homage to Freud's 1930 treatise of the same name.

Along with the talking cure, the novel draws inspiration from oral traditions of American storytelling, particularly the tall-tale[29] and the stand-up rantings of so-called "sicknik" comics like Lenny Bruce, Roth's claims to being funnier than Bruce notwithstanding (Nachman 420).[30] In interviews and essays, Roth has preferred to view his work in terms of Franz Kafka and canonical culture, but repeated reference in *Portnoy's Complaint* to comedians (124-125), radio personalities (161-164) and film stars (164-65) are convincing testimony to the author's indebtedness to American popular culture as well as Freudian thought.[31]

And this brings us back to food: In moments of overwhelming sexual desire, Portnoy resorts to what humor and sexuality scholar Gershon Legman called "food dirtying."[32] He masturbates into a candy wrapper (18) and a milk bottle (19). A cored apple – a Christian symbol of temptation – beckons young Alex. He falls "upon the orifice of the fruit, pretending that the cool and mealy hole was actually between the legs of that mythical being who always called me Big Boy" (19). That "mythical being" is his mother, Sophie, whom he calls "the most unforgettable character I've ever met" (1).

But the most infamous scenes in the novel center around Portnoy's auto-erotic misadventures with raw liver. Pornoy abuses

---

[29] See Guttmann 336.
[30] For more on the similarities between Lenny Bruce and the performative aspects of *Portnoy's Complaint*, see Grebstein 153.
[31] For Kafka reference, see Roth's "On Portnoy's Complaint" 21.
[32] See Legman's extensive catalogue of related dirty jokes in Volume II of his *Rationale of the Dirty Joke* (12.IV.2).

uncooked liver on two separate occasions: once behind a billboard on his way to a bar mitzvah lesson (19) and once in the privacy of his bathroom (150). The liver from the second episode later appears "on the end of a fork" at the family dinner table. Roth's choice of liver as the conduit for Portnoy's passions is significant. Liver is an *Ur*-Jewish food.[33] Interestingly, unlike other meats, it cannot be koshered merely by draining it of blood; liver must be split open and broiled. Under normal circumstances then, liver is an especially difficult meat to render fit for consumption.[34] Eating liver becomes all the more problematic after Portnoy wraps it around his own "little man" to achieve orgasm.

Freud believed that orality and sexuality were links on the same developmental chain toward ego formation. Of course, the relationship between gastronomy and sexuality had been established in Western culture long before Freud. Food and sexuality have been continually associated in Western art and literature – especially vis-à-vis the mythical power of aphrodisiacs. The linkage of food and sex with the image of the Jew is not new in modern literature either.[35] But for American-Jewish writers like Roth, food, fornication *and* family became the basic material of comic sketches.[36]

Orality and sexuality are inextricably linked for Portnoy with his mother. When he refuses to eat, Sophie threatens him with a "long bread knife…made of stainless steel, and […] little sawlike teeth" (16). This scene becomes the elemental memory of Portnoy's emasculation and is connected to the impotence for which he ultimately seeks psychiatric care. As an adolescent, his mother makes Portnoy promise to stop eating hamburgers and French fries (34-35). To Sophie, such all-American foods are *chazerai,*[37] sources of both physical and spiritual pollution. Portnoy rebels against his mother's many culinary prohibitions through masturbation: "… furiously I grab that battered battering

---

[33] Perhaps the most ubiquitous Anglo-Yiddishism is, "What am I? Chopped liver?"

[34] See Goodman for the history and possible Jewish origins of liver preparation.

[35] Both Joyce's *Ulysses* and Proust's *Remembrance of Things Past* pay significant attention to food, and both novels depict onanism.

[36] For more on this in *Portnoy's Complaint*, see Grebstein 162-163.

[37] In Hebrew, literally, the stuff of pigs.

ram to freedom [...] My wang was all I really had that I could call my own" (35). Auto-emancipation and auto-eroticism become one and the same for Portnoy.

Sophie's injunctions against contamination by food are matched by her single-minded fear that Portnoy will be preyed upon by the *shikses*[38] he so desperately ends up desiring. Her dread of unkosher food is tied to a past flirtation with a non-Jewish man: Sophie is haunted by the gastric distress she experienced after that man had coaxed her into eating a lobster dinner (101).[39] After Portnoy consumes his first lobster, he finds himself masturbating on a public bus next to the object of his desire – a *shikse* (87). Portnoy repeatedly, and often catastrophically, links food with sex. He learns to associate non-Jewish sex partners with syphilis – a condition he imagines will cause his penis to shrivel and fall on the kitchen floor with a "definite clink" (188). The kitchen is, of course, the sphere of his castrating mother.[40] He watches Sophie drain blood from meat (to render it kosher) and recalls an image of her menstrual blood (46-47). He connects the crime of eating his sister's chocolate pudding with his father's lust for a non-Jewish co-worker (97-98).

Portnoy's adolescent desire stirs in the presence of food: he follows "the fluttering yellow ringlets of a strange *shikse*" around a park and to a candy store, where she drinks hot chocolate with marshmallows (165). In college, he dates a non-Jewish woman whom he nicknames "The Pumpkin" (244). Portnoy's desire to consume *shikses* is inextricably bound up with his fetishization of food as objects of sexual gratification. He compulsively violates his mother's prohibitions on food and on assimilation. Embracing Sophie's twin taboos becomes a way for Portnoy to

---

[38] In Yiddish, literally, "a detested thing," a pejorative term for non-Jewish women.

[39] Crustaceans occupy an important place in the iconography of the Jewish comic experience of mainstream American culture – what we might call the "lobster melting pot." Woody Allen's *Annie Hall* (1977) includes an uproarious scene wherein a lobster runs away from comedy writer Alvy Singer (Allen) and his non-Jewish girlfriend, Annie (Diane Keaton). The narrator of *Inside, Outside* is a joke-writer who recalls his puzzlement when faced with his first lobster (Wouk 85). In an episode of the sitcom *Seinfeld*, "The Hamptons" (airdate May 12, 1994), to avenge an embarrassment George (Jason Alexander) prepares a lobster omelet for a kosher-keeping acquaintance.

[40] Portnoy imagines Sophie becoming hysterical at the sight of his diseased organ: "'His little thing,' screams my mother, 'that I used to tickle it to make him go wee-wee'" (189).

nourish his contempt of his mother and feed his antipathy for her values.

Portnoy's perspective on the Jewish middle class *parvenu* and the image of Jewish family life is, to say the least, insolent. He condemns his parents for making "us little Jewish boys believe ourselves to be [...] unique as unicorns on the one hand, geniuses and brilliant like nobody has ever been brilliant and beautiful before [...] saviors and sheer perfection on the one hand, and such bumbling, incompetent thoughtless, helpless, selfish [...] little *ingrates*, on the other" (133-134). This paradoxical stance mirrors the novel's own conflicted vision of Jewish distinctiveness. On the one hand, Roth portrays Jewish particularity as a source of ethical inspiration – Portnoy is New York City's assistant commissioner on human opportunity, "enemy of slumlords and bigots and rats" (120). On the other hand, he uses the novel to channel his wrath against bourgeois Jewish values, what Woody Allen once termed the dual divinities of God and carpeting. The novel blames particularism – identified in terms of dietary taboos, sexual proscriptions and fear of gentiles – for Jewish-American shortcomings, neuroses and frustrations.

Laughing at the Little Man

In 1972, Irving Howe issued his own disaffected complaint about the novel. In an essay titled "Philip Roth Reconsidered," Howe mocked: "The cruelest thing anyone can do with *Portnoy's Complaint* is to read it twice" (74).[41] His evident distaste for the novel can be traced back to the Holocaust – which for Howe, as noted earlier, marked the end of Jewish humor. *Portnoy's Complaint* spilled the seeds of important cultural capital. It had undermined "a wave of philo-Semitism [that] swept through our culture" following World War II and the revelations of Jewish suffering (Howe 76). Non-Jewish readers "could almost be heard breathing a sigh of relief, for it [*Portnoy's Complaint*] signaled an end to philo-Semitism in American culture, one no longer had

---

[41] While subsequent reads might not be as good as the first, even an adolescent Portnoy in the grips of masturbatory gusto would presumably have been able to think of something "crueler" to do with the novel than to reread it.

to listen to all that talk about Jewish morality, Jewish endurance, Jewish wisdom, Jewish families" (*ibid.*). What many consider the hallmark of Jewish humor, self-deprecation, Howe felt would actually decrease sympathy for Jews.

It is difficult now to sympathize with Howe's fear that the novel would herald a downturn in cordial relations with non-Jewish Americans. Distrust of Jews would surely have been more likely to stem from the high Jewish profile in the political and social turmoil accompanying the civil rights and anti-Vietnam movements, the sexual revolution or the Watergate scandal. Nor was *Portnoy's Complaint* the first pop-culture artifact to titillate American audiences with the shocking news that Jews were subject to the same strengths and weaknesses as everyone else. Lenny Bruce[42] had been famous since the late 1950s for performing Jewish-flavored material, using and misusing Yiddish words and frankly and sensationally discussing sexual, religious and racial issues in his act.

I believe the discomfort Howe expressed with Roth's novel reveals a frustration that post-*Portnoy*, Jewish Americans might no longer be able to claim superior morality, wisdom and familial warmth. Or, in Portnoy's words, that Jews might no longer be considered "unique as unicorns," "brilliant and beautiful," and "saviors and sheer perfection" (Roth 133). Instead, the novel portrayed Jews as "bumbling, incompetent...little *ingrates*" (134). Howe's *kvetch* boils down to this: Roth's exhibitionistic fantasy of the little man spoils the image of the Jew as ethical big-shot.

Yet Roth's own observations about Jewish humor in *Portnoy's Complaint* suggest he was no less serious about the comic image of the Jew in popular culture than Howe. At 33 – the same age as Jesus upon his death –Alex Portnoy hasn't outgrown his *schlemiel*hood; "the son struggl[es] to make the father understand" (8) his values by purchasing him a subscription to *Partisan Review.*[43] Roth presents a burlesque diminution of the Passion in the new Jerusalem of suburban New Jersey; there, the Jewish

---

[42] Already dead in 1969 and venerated by American intellectuals, including Howe himself, as a martyr to free speech.

[43] A publication Howe was associated with.

little man is crucified by his parents. Still considered by his mother
to be a baby (124), condescendingly referred to in public as her
"big boy" (126), Portnoy agonizes in the staccato delivery of a
stand-up comic: "A Jewish man with his parents alive is half the
time a helpless *infant*! [...] Spring me from this role I play of the
smothered son in the Jewish joke! Because it's beginning to pall
a little at thirty three! And also it *hoits*" (124). That Roth
references the *schlemiel* of jokes suggests this stock figure was
familiar to a wide American audience, and could serve as literary
short-hand for Jewish familial life with all its pressures and
responsibilities.

Portnoy despairs that his existence has taken on the form of a
borscht-belt gag: "'Help, help, my son the doctor is drowning!'
ha ha *ha*, ha ha *ha*, only what about the *pain* [...] What about the
guy [...] sinking beneath an ocean of parental relentlessness! [...]
I can't live any more in a world given its meaning and dimension
by some vulgar nightclub clown. By some – some *black
humorist!*" (125). Portnoy bemoans the fact that he is trapped in
a situation worthy of comedians Sam Levenson, Myron Cohen,
Henny Youngman and Milton Berle (*ibid*). Roth is playfully aware
that his representation of a young, Jewish male's neuroses parallels
the familiar exaggerations and stereotypes of Catskill *tummlers*,
or comics. The identification of Portnoy with a stock figure is
made even more explicit: "here's a joke for you, for instance.
Three Jews are walking down the street, my mother, my father
and me" (125). Portnoy envelopes his family life in the "set-up"
and "rule of three" that professional comedians use to structure
their jokes. The protagonist features himself as the punch line.

Incorporating explicit references to narrative strategies of
humor reveals the self-reflexivity of *Portnoy's Complaint*, which
in style and structure recalls a joke. Above the concluding lines
of the novel[44] appears the heading: "PUNCH LINE" (309). The
torrent of vituperation, confession and absurdity that Portnoy
reveals to Dr. Spielvogel serves as the perfect surrogate for the
comedian's monologue. Possibly Roth was influenced in his

---

[44] The only words, eight in total, not spoken by Portnoy himself.

composition by the neurotic routines of Chicago comedian Shelly Berman.[45] Saul Bellow's darkly humorous *The Last Analysis* may also have influenced Roth.[46] The Broadway play's central character is a once-popular comedian obsessed with psychoanalyzing himself in a kind of proto-"reality TV" show.

In the ironically titled penultimate chapter, "Exile," Roth shrewdly explores the dynamics of Jewish humor. Portnoy travels to Israel, where he meets Naomi, a young kibbutznik recently discharged from the army. Portnoy quickly confesses his love for her; she dismisses his proclamations as "silly jokes" (298). She probes a tender place in his psyche when she charges: "You seem to take some special pleasure, some pride, in making yourself the butt of your own peculiar sense of humor. [...] Everything you say is somehow always twisted, some way or another, to come out 'funny.' [...] everything is ironical or self-depreciating" (298-299). He corrects both her English and her character assessment, remarking that "self-deprecation is, after all, a classic form of Jewish humor" (299). Portnoy's understanding of the nature of Jewish humor echoes Freud's formulation. But Naomi rebuffs Portnoy's favorable view of self-deprecation. The idealistic, socialist Zionist labels him "nothing but a self-hating Jew" (300), insisting that his kind of humor is "[n]ot Jewish humor! No! *Ghetto* humor" (299).

And why doesn't Naomi tolerate self-mockery? Because, Portnoy counters, "It was Diaspora Jews just like myself who had gone by the millions to the gas chambers without ever raising a hand against their persecutors [...]" (299). Naomi, filtered through Portnoy, sounds a note of indignation similar to the one Irving Howe directed at Roth. Not only does the passage quoted above reflect a view of self-mocking humor as forbidden in the post-Auschwitz world; it also links Jewish self-deprecation to self-destruction. Inveterate masturbator Alex Portnoy is ultimately defined by self-abuse.

---

[45] By 1963, Berman had sold millions of albums and perfected his trademark one-sided telephone conversation skits that framed his anxious take on modern life. His routines may themselves owe some narrative debt to the "Cohen on the Telephone" acts popular in the early part of the 20th century.

[46] On this point, see Goldman (1971) 246.

Naomi goes on to call him a *schlemiel* (300). Enraged by the insult, Portnoy tries to rape her, but finds himself again incapacitated – his "little man" refuses to rise to her challenge. Disdainful of his weakness, Naomi echoes Sophie's refrain: "This *son!* This *boy!* This *baby!*" (303). As an adult, Portnoy found far more than 50 ways to leave his liver, but in his self-loathing, Portnoy reverts to an obsession with oral stimulation (305). Incapable of achieving an erection, he becomes "the slavish mouth that can satisfy a woman" (305). Only to "Eat!" he exclaims, "this banquet walking the streets" (305-306).

Portnoy's existence is an absurdity, his Jewish distinctiveness a curse and his particular sensibilities – what Spielvogel diagnosed as "strongly-felt ethical and altruistic impulses [...] perpetually warring with extreme sexual longings" – remain difficult to reconcile with the values of his youth (epigraph). The figure of the Jew is represented in Roth's novel by the comic sad sack, the bumbling loser who will humiliate himself to beat the world to the punch(line). In 1969, the literary image of the Jew was epitomized by the character of Alex Portnoy.

The Little Man Comes of Age

Nearly 30 years later, first-time screenwriter Adam Herz wrote *American Pie* based, in part, on his experiences growing up in suburban East Grand Rapids, Michigan. The movie is a relatively smart and sympathetic take on the teen sex-comedy genre initiated by the success of writer-director Bob Clark's 1981 hit, *Porky's*— a film franchise with the most unkosher of titles. The plot of teen sex comedies invariably revolves around a male's attempt to lose his virginity and thereby attain manhood. Soon after its 1999 release, several notorious scenes catapulted *American Pie* into pop-culture fame.

The central figure in the film – and its sequels, *American Pie II* (2001) and *American Wedding* (2003) – is the hapless James Emmanuel Levinstein who is Jewish in name only. Among his friends Levinstein is called Jim or Jimbo. Jim[47] is a clear example

---

[47] Played by the non-Jewish actor Jason Biggs.

of the *schlemiel*, "innocent, impotent and weak" (Wisse 9). There are no outward signs of Jim's Jewishness other than his patronymic. But his parents exhibit a stifling dynamic of support and burdensome unmanning which endows him with the same boy-man traits Alex Portnoy laments in himself. Jim's father[48] is a caricature of the nerdy parent who means well, but always embarrasses his son with his square vocabulary and painfully out-of-touch lectures on sex. He is a less threatening, but equally mortifying, parallel to Sophie Portnoy.

Herz's original screenplay for *American Pie* is clearly indebted to Roth's novel and evinces a similar connection between food and sexuality. The most memorable scene in *American Pie* features Jim masturbating with a warm pie left by his mother on the kitchen counter. Alongside it, a pink note inscribed with a heart reads: "Apple – your favorite!!! Enjoy – Mom." With his pants at his ankles and pelvis thrusting madly into the pie, Jim's culinary coitus is interrupted when his father returns unexpectedly and catches him *in flagrent delicto*. Apple pie, of course, is one third of the secular American trinity completed by baseball and hotdogs.[49]

The film presents Jim as a fully assimilated Jewish central character. The fact that he demonstrates characteristics of both the physically clumsy *schlemiel* and the existentially unlucky *shlimazel* is not linked to his Jewishness in the screenplay.[50] Nonetheless, Jim's character owes much to the comic figure of the Jewish little man, even if his particularity has been all but effaced. Portnoy, the distinctive Jew and marginalized *schlemiel*, has been transformed into Jim, a fully acculturated American whose *shlemiel*dom seems more due to nature than nurture. As for the object of infatuation, Herz substitutes the down-home symbol of Americana – apple pie – for Roth's typically Jewish liver.

Both *Portnoy's Complaint* and *American Pie* portray sexual odysseys. Portnoy seeks a cure for his impotence, while Jim seeks

---

[48] Played by the veteran Jewish comic actor Eugene Levy.
[49] Incidentally, Jim and his friends gather several times in the film at their hangout – a hot-dog joint where they are shown consuming copious quantities of wieners.
[50] For a discussion of these two archetypes combined in one character, see Boyer.

to lose his virginity and reclaim his dignity after an embarrassing episode of premature ejaculation, captured via webcam, is broadcast on the Internet. Both characters' sexual journeys are attempts to regain or to attain manhood. Portnoy flees from his mother's castrating presence, and Jim from the humiliating emasculation visited upon him by his father.[51]

Jewish food preferences help to perpetuate religious and ethnic distinctiveness. On a practical level, religious laws governing food consumption can serve as boundaries to social interaction with other ethnic groups. As the American-Jewish community loses traditional food preferences *and* as Jewish foods are adopted by other groups, we can expect that one crucial factor of identity will vanish. The move from Portnoy's liver to Jim's all-American apple pie – from the guilt-ridden domain of home cooking and nice Jewish girls to the blithe pursuit of *chazerai* and *shikses* – reflects a larger shift in American culture. The absorption of Jews into the American mainstream is mirrored by the pervasiveness of the Jewish influence on American humor. However, when cultural identity breaks down – when *Yiddishkeit*[52] becomes, in effect, *Yiddish*-lite – then recognizably Jewish humor may disappear as well.

During a period of unprecedented cultural and social opportunity, Roth evoked the tensions of a Jewish identity divided against itself, equally despairing of both marginality and assimilation. *Portnoy's Complaint* may have been the climax of Jewish humor in America; *American Pie* may merely reveal Jewish humor's descent into *post coitum triste*. Jewish humor in America is primarily about the anxiety of difference and the anxiety of

---

[51] In *American Wedding,* the final installment of the trilogy, Jim's Jewishness – or his lack thereof – is addressed directly. His future father-in-law, Harold Flaherty (Fred Willard), toasts the young couple's happiness with the hope that the two families will "celebrate many *shivas* together." The Levinstein family squirms slightly at Flaherty's malapropism, but they clink glasses and drink. For some members of the Levinstein family, the *simcha* (festival) of *American Wedding* may just as well be a *shiva* (wake). When Jim's paternal grandmother meets his red-haired fiancée, Michele Flaherty (Alyson Hannigan), the atmosphere is anything but celebratory. Grandma (Angela Paton) rises from her wheelchair, points an accusing finger at Jim's Irish rose, and cries out: "Not Jewish! Not Jewish! *Goya!*" Her outburst (representing retrograde attitudes opposing assimilation) threatens to disrupt the wedding and introduces a ludicrous sub-plot. Grandma learns to accept Jim's interfaith marriage after she mistakenly has sex with Jim's priapic pal, Stiffler (Sean William Scott). Once again, physical intercourse is the key to smooth social intercourse, even for those clinging to Old World values.

[52] In Yiddish, "Jewishness."

losing this particularity. When such anxieties are replaced by complacence, we can expect Jewish humor to be reduced to the suburban foibles of Jim Levinstein, a crypto-*schlemiel* who has probably never heard a word of Yiddish in his Midwestern life. *Apropos* Woody Allen's remark that comedy is a meringue, we might say that Jewish humor in the 21st century is as American as apple pie. The little man has now become an American folk hero – or, even more symbolic of Jewish integration, we might say that the Jewish little man has become an American everyman.

The shocking bile of Portnoy's liver episode has been replaced in our day with the saccharine of *American Pie*'s ritual laughter. With another generation grown and questions of assimilation muted, *American Pie* dishes out Portnoy's leftovers. In 1969, Alex Portnoy announced that he would "*conquer* America" (265) through his sexual appetite and mania for oral coitus. Thirty years later, the virginal Jim Levinstein is condemned to feast on the scraps of an already-devoured promised land. Cultural security and economic prosperity come at a cost: American-Jewish humor can't have its pie and eat it too.

From Little Man to Hit Man?

The Jewish presence in American humor has shifted in the last century. In vaudeville, then Broadway, and later in radio, film, television and stand-up, Jews were the talent behind the comedy. They were the writers, performers and actors. In the 1950s, many comics, like Jack Benny and George Burns, adopted non-Jewish names and steered clear of Jewish references in their work. Then in the 1960s, according to Albert Goldman, Jewish humor became the bread-and-butter of comedy (*Freakshow* 170). Jewish cultural assimilation may be so complete now and the influence of Jews on American humor so pervasive, that an identifiable Jewish comic sensibility will soon be a thing of the past. Jewish humor is now as ubiquitous and de-ethnicized as bagel shops. If Koreans in midtown and Midwesterners on Main Street can spread a *shmear,*[53] Jews will no longer be the only ones who get to *shpritz.*[54]

---

[53] In Yiddish, "smear," as in cream cheese.
[54] In Yiddish, "to spray, squirt."

My conclusion has been echoed by recent alarmist articles in Jewish publications. In October 2002, *Moment* magazine wondered whether Jews are still funny.[55] A survey conducted by the University of Hertfordshire's Laughlab, associated with the British Association for the Advancement of Science, asked more than 2 million people worldwide to rate 40,000 jokes. Not one Jewish joke made the list of the funniest, prompting from the *Forward* the *geshrei*[56], "Is this a Joke?"

Of course, Jewish artists whose work is characterized by comic stylings continue to have their place at the American table. Young writers, such as Nathan Englander and Helen Schulman; Hollywood fixtures such as Woody Allen and even Adam Sandler; and comedians such as Jerry Seinfeld and the up-and-coming Sarah Silverman make use of distinctly Jewish material and character types. The successes of assimilation may merely signal the creation of new forms of humor that acknowledge Jewish inclusion while nodding to some traits signifying the last vestiges of cultural difference. Recent years may, in fact, have witnessed a metamorphosis of Jewish humor that would stand Popkin's little-man-who-isn't-there thesis on its head.

The enormously popular HBO television series, *The Sopranos*, features the courthouse trials and back-room tribulations of an Italian-American mafia family. Both pathos and bathos are combined as the Sopranos navigate suburban American life in scenes that swing wildly between farce and brutal violence. The crime family's squabbles and their domestic discord owe an unacknowledged debt to the Portnoy family. Mob boss Tony Soprano (James Gandolfini) is from the Old Country of New Jersey, just like Alex Portnoy (and Philip Roth); Tony suffers from panic attacks (so, reportedly, does Roth); and in almost every episode he is shown seeking treatment with a psychiatrist. The source of Tony's psychological troubles is his mother Livia (Nancy Marchand), an overbearing, vindictive, guilt-mongering maternal figure who makes Sophie Portnoy look like mother-of-the-year.

An episode from the third season, "Fortunate Son" (airdate

---

[55] See the article by Epstein.
[56] In Yiddish, "a cry of despair."

March 11, 2001) written by Scott A. Kessler, reveals that Tony's panic attacks are brought on by deli slices of cappicola ham. He links an awareness of his parents' sexuality with the weekly delivery of meat from the local butcher (whom his mobster father periodically shook down). Tony's mother was only in a good mood, he says, when the meat arrived; it was "probably the only time the old man got laid." As in *Portnoy's Complaint*, talk therapy exposes a psychopathology linking food to sex and a domineering maternal presence. "Pretty sick, huh? – getting turned on by free cold cuts," Tony confesses to his psychiatrist. Dr. Melfi (Lorraine Bracco) likens the memory to Proust's madeleine. Instead of liver or apple pie, *The Sopranos* substitutes cappicola ham, insisting on ethnic distinctiveness by way of "tribal" food.[57]

Might Tony Soprano be the sort of man Portnoy wishes to be – free from ethical and altruistic impulses, free to indulge in his sexual gratification without fear of retribution? Alas, Tony is not entirely free; like Portnoy, he continually cowers under the castrating shadow of his mother, even after her death. Tony Soprano may really be a *marrano*, a hidden Jew, although his character is hardly Wisse's "innocent, impotent and weak" *schlemiel*. Tony's possession of traits traditionally associated with the comic image of the Jew suggests that beneath the coarse exterior, he is a little man struggling to find his place in an overwhelming world. In terms of the image of the Jew in popular culture, Tony Soprano may merely be "passing" as Italian.

Rather than become de-Semitized, as Popkin believed, perhaps popular culture has become Semitized to such a degree that an Italian mob boss can now become a figure of uneasy hilarity, functioning much like the comic image of the Jew. The Jewish little man, so prevalent in modern American humor, may have paved the way for the acceptance of other comic figures of excluded groups, be they black, Latino, female, homosexual or Italian.

---

[57] The importance of food to the television series is apparent from the popular *Sopranos Family Cookbook*. Needless to say, there is no *Portnoy's Complaint* or *American Pie* cookbook.

The Little Man's Last Stand?

Writer Ben Hecht complained in 1944 that a "generation has grown up without having seen or heard of a Jew – except as a massacre victim or world menace" (qtd. in Romeyn and Kugelmass 50-51). This is no longer the case. The image of the Jew in America is not that of victim, nor that of villain. The spectacular success of Jewish comedians, comic actors and writers has entrenched the image of the Jew as the quintessential little man, and the little man as an American hero. Even recent films from America and abroad that depict the Jew as "massacre victim" have employed the *schlemiel* archetype – think of films like Roberto Benigni's *Life Is Beautiful* and *Jakob the Liar,* starring Robin Williams.

It is striking how many commentators have based their assessments of the fate of Jewish humor on a consideration of the Holocaust. Then again, as humor scholar Elliott Oring noted, prophesies regarding the fate of Jewish humor really express an anxiety over the disappearance of Jewish identity (271). Kristol and Howe both felt that Jewish humor came to an end with the Holocaust. Popkin blamed Hitler for the banishment of visibly Jewish characters from American arts and entertainment. Rosenberg and Shapiro implied that Nazism staunched the assimilation of American Jewry. And Philip Roth invoked the gas chambers to complicate the naïve acceptance of a fundamentally self-deprecating Jewish sense of humor.

Given the subject of humor, it may seem odd that the crimes of the Holocaust have been invoked so frequently by critics. Recall, however, that the concept of Jewish humor has traditionally been grounded in adversity and Jewish suffering. In his important article from 1983, "The People of the Joke: On the Conceptualization of a Jewish Humor," Oring persuasively argued that because Jews have suffered exceedingly and yet have continued to laugh, it stands to reason "… *that the humor of the Jews must in some way be distinctive from other humors which are not born of despair*" (267, emphasis in original). He concluded: "The notion of Jewish humor will persist as long as there remain conceptualizations that fundamentally distinguish

Jewish history and experience from the history and experience of a world of nations" (*ibid*). As the Holocaust recedes in time, and as other genocides and atrocities hold the world's attention, perhaps one previously vital distinction between Jewish history and the history of other peoples may be blurred. The proliferation of comic literary treatments of the Holocaust and its survivors may be a symptom of this change.[58]

The history of Jews in America has not been characterized by overwhelming suffering and persecution. So it is difficult to distinguish Jewish experience from the experience of other ethnic groups able to blend easily with the majority culture. In America, Jewish identity, at least as reflected in popular culture, has become inseparable from the image of the Jew as both comic *schlemiel* and comic genius. Jewish humor may be the last vestige of identity that remains for younger generations of secular, assimilated American Jews. The dearth of self-consciously Jewish elements in *American Pie* and its sequels, films clearly indebted to *Portnoy's Complaint* and long-standing conceptions of Jewish humor, is significant. Rather than merely signaling the assimilation of the Jewish little man, popular culture may now be recording the vanishing American Jew.

---

[58] Some examples of the broad range of humor related to the Holocaust in American work that I find particularly interesting include: Saul Bellow's *Mr. Sammler's Planet*, Nathan Englander's "The Tumblers," Jonathan Safran Foer's *Everything is Illuminated*, portions of Marcie Hershman's *Tales of the Master Race*, Arthur Miller's short story "The Performer," Cynthia Ozick's *Rosa*, Francine Prose's *Guided Tours of Hell*, Philip Roth's *The Ghost Writer* and his short story "Eli, the Fanatic," Helen Schulman's *The Revisionist*, and Lore Segal's *Her First American*.

Works Cited

Alter, Robert. "Jewish Humor and the Domestication of Myth." *Veins of Humor*. Ed. Harry Levin. Cambridge, MA: Harvard University Press, 1972.

Altman, Sig. *The Comic Image of the Jew: Explorations of Pop Culture Phenomenon*. Rutherford, NJ: Fairleigh Dickinson UP, 1971.

Arendt, Hannah. "The Jew as Pariah: A Hidden Tradition." *The Jew as Pariah*. Ed. Ron Feldman. New York: Grove Press, 1978.

Bakhtin, Mikhail. *Rabelais and His World*. Trans. Hélène Iswolsky. Bloomington, IN: Indiana University Press, 1984.

Bellow, Saul. *The Last Analysis*. New York: Viking Press, 1965.

Ben-Amos, Dan. "The 'Myth' of Jewish Humor." *Western Folklore* 32.2 (1973): 112-131.

Berger, Arthur Asa. *Jewish Jesters: A Study in American Popular Comedy*. Cresskill, NJ: Hampton Press, 2001.

—. *The Genius of the Jewish Joke*. Northvale, NJ: Jason Aronson, 1997.

Boyer, Jay. "The *Schlemiezel*: Black Humor and the *Shtetl* Tradition." *Semites and Stereotypes*. Eds. Avner Ziv and Anat Zajdman. Westport, CT: Greenwood Press, 1993.

Chase, Jefferson. *Inciting Laughter: The Development of 'Jewish Humor' in 19th Century German Culture*. New York: Walter De Gruyter, 2000.

Cohen, Sarah Blacher. "The Jewish Literary Comediennes." *Comic Relief: Humor in Contemporary American Literature*. Ed. Sarah Blacher Cohen. Urbana, IL: University of Illinois Press, 1978.

Davies, Christie. "Exploring the Thesis of the Self-deprecating Jewish Sense of Humor." *Humor* 4-2 (1991): 189-209.

—. "An Explanation of Jewish Jokes about Jewish Women." *Humor* 3-4 (1990): 363-378.

Dundes, Alan. "A Study of Ethnic slurs: The Jew and the Polack in the United States." *Journal of American Folklore* 84 (332): 186-203.

Eastman, Max. *The Sense of Humor*. New York: Charles Scribner's, 1936.

Epstein, Lawrence. "Are Jews Still Funny?" *Moment* (October 2002): 62-66, 86-89.

—. *The Haunted Smile*. New York: Public Affairs, 2001.

Fisher, Seymour and Rhoda L. *Pretend the World Is Funny and Forever: A Psychological Analysis of Comedians, Clowns, and Actors*. Hillsdale, NJ: Lawrence Erlbaum Assoc., 1981.

Friedman, Hershey. "Is There Humor in the Hebrew Bible? A Rejoinder." *Humor*. 15-2 (2002): 215-222.

Friedman, Hershey. "Humor in the Hebrew Bible." *Humor*. 13-3 (2000): 257-285.

Freud, Sigmund. *Jokes and Their Relation to the Unconscious* [1905]. Trans. James Strachey. New York: Norton, 1963.

Gilman, Sander. *Jewish Self-Hatred: Anti-Semitism and the Hidden Language of the Jews*. Baltimore: Johns Hopkins University Press, 1986.

Goldman, Albert. "Laughtermakers." *Jewish Wry: Essays on Jewish Humor*. Ed. Sarah Blacher Cohen. Bloomington, IN: Indiana University Press, 1987.

—. *Freakshow*. New York: Atheneum, 1971.

Goodman, Matthew. "What Am I, Chopped Liver? Truth Is, It Could Always Be Worse." *Forward* (6 December 2002): 13.

Grebstein, Sheldon. "The Comic Anatomy of *Portnoy's Complaint*." *Comic Relief Humor in Contemporary American Literature*. Ed. Sarah Blacher Cohen. Urbana, IL: University of Illinois Press, 1978.

Gross, Max. "Is This a Joke? Jewish Humor Fails to Make List of Funniest Jests." *Forward* 25 October 2002. <http://www.forward.com/issues/2002/02.10.25/fast3html>.

Grotjahn, Martin. "Jewish Jokes and their Relation to Masochism." *A Celebration of Laughter*. Ed. Werner Mendel. Los Angeles: Mara, 1970.

Guttman, Allen. "Jewish Humor." *The Comic Imagination in American Literature*. Ed. Louis Rubin, Jr. New Brunswick, NJ: Rutgers University Press, 1973.

Heine, Heinrich. *Deutschland: A Winter's Tale*. Trans., Ed. T.J. Reed. London: Angel Books, 1997.

Herz, Adam (screenplay). *American Pie*. Dir. Chris Weitz, Paul Weitz. USA, 1999.

Howe, Irving. "Philip Roth Reconsidered." *Commentary* 54 (1972): 69-77.

—. "The Nature of Jewish Laughter." *Jewish Wry*. Ed. Sarah Blacher Cohen. Bloomington, IN: Indiana University Press, 1987.

Janus, Samuel. "The Great Jewish-American Comedians' Identity Crisis." *The American Journal of Psychoanalysis*. Vol. 40. No. 3. (1980): 259-265.

Joyce, James. *Ulysses*. New York: Vintage Books, 1961.

Kristol, Irving. "Is Jewish Humor Dead?" *Commentary* 12 (1951): 431-436.

LeBlanc, Ronald. "Love and Death and Food." *Literature and Film Quarterly* 17.1 (1989): 18-26.

Legman, Gershon. *Rationale of the Dirty Joke* V.II. New York: Breaking Point, 1975.

Lipman, Steve. *Laughter in Hell: The Use of Humor During the Holocaust*. Northvale, NJ: Jason Aronson, 1991.

Madison, Charles. *Yiddish Literature: Its Scope and Major Writers*. New York: Frederick Ungar, 1968.

Markfield, Wallace. "The Yiddishization of American Humor." *Esquire* 64 (Oct. 1965): 114-115,136).

Morreal, John. "Sarcasm, irony, wordplay, and humor in the Hebrew Bible: A response to Hershey Friedman." *Humor* 14-3 (2001): 293-301.

Nachman, Gerald. *Seriously Funny: The Rebel Comedians of the 1950's and 1960's*. New York: Pantheon Books, 2003.

Novak, William and Moshe Waldoks, Eds. *The Big Book of Jewish Humor*. New York: HarperCollins, 1981.

Oring, Elliott. "The People of the Joke: On the Conceptualization of a Jewish Humor." *Western Folklore*. Vol. XLII No. 4 October (1983): 261-271.

Popkin, Henry. "The Vanishing Jew of Our Popular Culture: The Little Man Who is No Longer There." *Commentary* July (1952): 46-55.

Reik, Theodor. *Jewish Wit.* New York: Gamut Press, 1962.

Romeyn, Esther and Jack Kugelmass, Eds. *Let There Be Laughter! Jewish Humor in America.* Chicago: Spertus Press, 1997.

Rosenberg, Bernard and Gilbert Shapiro. "Marginality and Jewish Humor." *Midstream.* Spring (1958): 70-80.

Rosenblatt, Gary. "Mel Brooks' 2,000-Year-Old Man Act Gets a Fresh Spin." *New York Jewish Week* 16 January 1998. 10 August 2003 <http://www.jwishsf.com/bk980116/etspin.htm>

Rosenfeld, Isaac. "Adam and Eve on Delancey Street." *Commentary* VIII (October 1949): 385-387.

Roskies, David. "Laughing off the Trauma of History." *Prooftexts* 2.1 (1982): 53-77.

Roth, Philip. "On Portnoy's Complaint." *Reading Myself and Others.* New York: Farrar

Straus and Giroux, 1975.

—. *Portnoy's Complaint.* New York: Bantam Books, 1970.

—. "Civilization and Its Discontents." *New American Review.* Ed. Theodore Solotaroff. New York: New American Library, 1968: (7-81).

Saroglou, Vassilis. "Religion and Sense of Humor: An A Priori Incompatibility?" *Humor* 15-2 (2002): 191-214.

Shechner, Mark. "Philip Roth." *Partisan Review* 41 (1974): 410-427.

Stora-Sandor, Judith. "The Stylistic Metamorphosis of Jewish Humor." *Humor* 4-2 (1991): 211-222.

Whitfield, Stephen. "The Distinctiveness of American Jewish Humor." *Modern Judaism* 6 (1986): 245-260.

—. "Laughter in the Dark: Notes on American Jewish Humor." *Midstream* 24.2 (1978): 48-58.

Wisse, Ruth. *The Modern Jewish Canon: A Journey Through Language and Culture.* New York: The Free Press, 2000.

—. *The Schlemiel as Modern Hero.* Chicago: University of Chicago Press, 1971.

Wouk, Herman. *Inside, Outside*. Boston: Little, Brown and Co., 1985.

Yates, Norris. *The American Humorist: Conscience of the Twentieth Century*. Ames, IA: Iowa State UP, 1964.

Ziv, Avner. "Introduction." *Humor* 4-2 (1991): 145-148.

Chapter Four

POLITICS:
"Lessons" of the
Holocaust

By Michael E. Staub

How have the lessons of the Holocaust – its meaning and possible political implications – changed from the end of World War II to the present? It's a deceptively simple question. In the fields of American literature and popular culture, extensive scholarship has focused on representations of the Holocaust (including on television and in film). But the role of Holocaust consciousness in American-Jewish politics – particularly the political battles *within* the American-Jewish community – has received far less attention. And what little scrutiny there has been – for example, in general overviews of American-Jewish history – often rests on false premises. In this in-depth exploration of the political context of Holocaust consciousness, I will argue that conventional wisdom about both the timing and the content of Holocaust consciousness, among other things, needs revision.

My main objective, however, is to demonstrate the richness of earlier discussions – now forgotten – of the Holocaust's potential lessons. The erasure from collective memory of earlier debates has tremendous consequences for contemporary American-Jewish life. By paying attention to conflicts *among* American Jews, rather than assuming they spoke with one voice, we gain a deepened understanding of our history and of our contributions to the wider American culture.

A Forgotten Story

It is widely assumed that in the immediate postwar era, there was almost no mention in American public life of the Nazi genocide; indeed it is simply stated as self-evident that the Holocaust was not a reference point for American-Jewish politics until the 1960s. On this point, conservatives and liberals generally agree. For instance, *Commentary* senior editor Gabriel Schoenfeld writes in 1999, "it is striking to recall that in the first decade and a half after World War II, the destruction of Europe's Jews was a subject shrouded in taboo and seldom discussed in public or print." This silence, he continues, only "began to dissipate in the 1960s, first with the trial of Adolf Eichmann in Israel in 1961, and then with the Six Day War in June 1967" (Schoenfeld A25). Historian Peter Novick makes similar assumptions. On the first page of his 1999 book, *The Holocaust in American Life,* Novick states categorically that the Nazi genocide of European Jewry was "hardly talked about for the first 20 years or so after World War II" (Novick 1).

In fact, the Holocaust was frequently invoked in American public discussion. Far from being silent – either out of horror at the magnitude of the Nazi crimes or out of respectful sensitivity toward the trauma of survivors – commentators of all political persuasions repeatedly made analogies to the mass murder of European Jewry when debating domestic political issues or explaining its purported "lessons" for America.[1]

---

[1] This habit of drawing "lessons" may, in hindsight, seem insensitive: contemporary observers have become more attuned to the Holocaust's horrific specificities and the inappropriateness of facile comparisons. Many thoughtful commentators now insist that lesson-making of all kinds is impossible and a dishonor to the dead. Such sensibilities were not, however, operative for much of the postwar period. The notion that it might be indecent to engage in comparisons or analogies was not articulated until the late 1960s.

After the ghastly revelations of 1945, the Nazi genocide of European Jews was invoked almost at once in debates over American politics. By the mid-1960s, assumptions about the lessons of Nazism for American political life had, in fact, gone through at least three distinct stages.

An Overview

In early sections of this chapter, I chart the role of political invocations of the Holocaust before the Six Day War. It is especially valuable to focus attention on this period because the summer of 1967 is generally taken to be the moment when the Holocaust, as a political reference point, really burst into public American life. An examination of periodical literature from the years immediately after 1945, however, indicates that political commentary (especially in the Jewish press) made frequent reference to the Holocaust, particularly in the context of the civil rights movement.

As they had already done during World War II, both left-wing and liberal American Jews continued to develop equivalencies between German Nazism and American anti-black racism after 1945. They often identified directly with African Americans; in a racist and anti-Semitic environment – the logic went – Jews, by helping blacks, were also helping themselves. When the Cold War undermined that analogy as un-American, a new analogy between Nazism and Stalinism grew in its place.

In the late 1950s, a second form of Holocaust consciousness emerged. Inspired by the Reform rabbis' movement for "prophetic Judaism" and led by committed Zionists within the American Jewish Congress, antiracist activists began to argue that if they did not help blacks, American Jews would be no better than the German people who had done nothing to prevent the Holocaust. This line of reasoning came to full flowering in the early 1960s, which also saw the beginnings of a third (more particularist) strand of argumentation: one which identified the most important lesson of the Holocaust as the need for Jews to protect themselves and fight for their own survival.

The remainder of this chapter takes the story of Holocaust

consciousness in American political life through the tumultuous 1960s to the present day. It lingers a while in the 1960s and '70s because that era's reconfigurations of Jewish identity had such a lasting influence. Many of the current views on the lessons of the Holocaust and the proper way to honor the memory of the dead were first advanced then.

In the 1960s and 1970s, the turn toward a more survivalist interpretation of Jewish identity was especially evident in discussions of American Jewry's relationship to Israel and in debates over Jewish reproductive levels. Further Holocaust lessons were identified and contested in this context. The right-wing Jewish Defense League, formed in 1968 during the height of the New Left student rebellions, became influential far beyond its modest numbers. The JDL slogan "Never Again" became shorthand for the idea that henceforth Jews refused to be on the receiving end of violence, but also that violence could now, however regretfully, be embraced as a necessary component of Jewish pride. Realpolitik should replace idealism.

At the same time, in reaction to both the sexual revolution and Jewish involvement in black civil rights and anti-Vietnam War activism, Orthodox leaders grew increasingly outspoken, particularly on the subject of Jewish fertility rates. They, too, became influential far beyond the numbers of their adherents. Orthodox leaders developed the argument – which in the 1970s was taken up by Jews across the religious and ideological spectrum – that a key lesson of the Holocaust was the need for Jewish women to bear more children.

I conclude with an examination of the current state of Holocaust consciousness in American political life. In the 1980s and 1990s, both scholarly knowledge and general awareness of the Holocaust advanced exponentially over what was known and understood a generation earlier. Even so, contemporary politicians and media commentators continue to make facile references to the Holocaust to dramatize or promote various political agendas.

Already in the 1960s and '70s, the Holocaust had become a kind of *lingua franca* of intracommunal contest, in which American Jews slammed each other with ever more reductive analogies. Young Jewish radicals arrested in a synagogue while staging a Vietnam War protest later accused the rabbi of behaving no better than the *Judenrat*[2] in a Nazi-controlled ghetto. On the other hand, when Breira, a center-left coalition of rabbis and intellectuals working toward a peaceful resolution of the Middle East crisis in the early 1970s, called on Israel to help establish a sovereign Palestinian state, a right-wing commentator criticized the group for "acting as the 'Yudenrat' in the Nazi concentration camps where my family perished" (Riz 5). In 1969, Harvard sociologist Nathan Glazer drew parallels between student radicals and Nazis, writing: "the New Left likes final victories and final solutions" (Glazer 34).

There is another important aspect to the wranglings of these earlier decades. Because simplistic and spurious lesson-making remains pervasive, it is especially worthwhile and valuable to reconstruct the history of this practice. Earlier phases of the debate are erased from view when modern commentators blithely repeat the myth that Jews were largely silent about the Holocaust in the postwar period. By revisiting earlier phases in intra-Jewish communal conflict, we see how earnestly and seriously American Jews wrestled with the immensely painful and seemingly contradictory lessons of the Holocaust.

As we recover this history, we find unexpected conjunctions. For example, we discover that passionate Zionism and involvement in the civil rights struggle were considered strongly compatible in the 1950s and early 1960s. We recover unexpected intensity and complexity in the debate over what – in ethnic, spiritual and political terms – a Jewish identity might contain. And we revise our present-day presumptions about what key concepts – among them assimilation and adherence to tradition, self-hatred and self-affirmation – used to mean. Each of these concepts was at one time subject to fierce contest as American Jews sought to sort out what they owed themselves, each other and other Americans in the post-Holocaust era.

---

[2] German for "Jewish council." During World War II, Nazi authorities required ghettos to form a *Judenrat* to take on the duties of a local government. These councils acted as intermediaries to carry out oppressive dictates, such as providing forced labor battalions for German war factories, and eventually delivering Jews to the trains bound for death camps.

The Immediate Postwar Years

In the war's aftermath, the Nazi genocide of European Jewry became a topic for discussion in American-Jewish political life almost at once. Commentators agreed that the Nazi genocide was a logical reference point from which to draw conclusions about contemporary social issues in the United States. Leading Jewish liberal periodicals in the immediate postwar era were especially receptive to the analogy between German fascism and American racism. For instance, after race riots "directed against the presence of Negro students in racially mixed schools" broke out in several northern cities in late 1945, the Labor Zionist publication *Jewish Frontier* observed that those "familiar with the rise of Nazism [would immediately recognize] most of the white troublemakers [as] boys with bad scholarship and attendance marks, the perfect Hitler material" (Cahnman 16, 18).

Early Jewish commentary did not hesitate to draw direct lessons from "a Nazi extermination program" in order "to explain a southern lynching." Leo Pfeffer, a prominent lawyer on the staff of the American Jewish Congress's Commission on Law and Social Action, wrote in 1946 that "as Hitler well knew, [a lie] will be believed, no matter how big it is, if only it is repeated often enough." So too, the "continued repetition of the fairy tale that Negro blood is different from and inferior to Caucasian has caused millions of uneducated or partially educated poor whites to consider Negroes an intermediate species between simian and human" (Pfeffer 6). In the same way, ordinary German citizens had

> participated or acquiesced in mass murder of Jews because for years they had been exposed to the lie that the Jews were their enemy and that all would be well when Jewish blood would flow. Race libels do not usually have immediate recognizable results, but their cumulative effect when compared with defamation of individuals is as atomic fission to the explosion of a fire-cracker (Pfeffer 6).

The new journal *Commentary*, sponsored by the American

Jewish Committee, repeatedly invoked a Nazi analogy to dramatize its disapproval of racial discrimination, especially in housing and employment practices. A 1947 essay in *Commentary* entitled "Homes for Aryans Only" put a distinctly American spin on the possible lessons of Nazism. The author argued that a libertarian tradition did not give American property owners a legal right to refuse to sell their homes to "non-Caucasians" (including Jews). Rhetorically linking the emancipation of slaves with the liberation of European Jewry, the author wrote: "Eighty years after Gettysburg, and two years after Hitler, the proposition that all men are created equal is again being whittled down, and in the area perhaps most crucial for a future democratic America – the area of our neighborhood life" (Abrams 421).

A 1948 essay in *Commentary* – with the ominous title, "Alaska's Nuremberg Laws" – attacked that state's legislation, directed at Indians, permitting the seizure of "the possessions of Americans solely because they belong to a minority race" (Cohen 136). Though the magazine had begun to articulate the Cold War liberal attitudes soon to blossom within its pages, in 1948 *Commentary* could still, with regard to race relations, stress the "painful theme" of an American "double standard" after the victory over fascism.

> In the aftermath of World War II it became apparent that segregated war memorials and pre-war Jim Crow patterns would not be submissively accepted as the fruits of democratic victory. These resentments have deepened. In a world-wide war against Nazism the survival of racism in America undercut our propaganda and caricatured our liberations. The anomaly is no less devastating in an era of new political conflict between democratic and totalitarian symbols – especially since the contemporary commissars officially reject the racism which the brown-shirts proclaimed (Wechslers 304).

For at least a few years, the Nazi genocide became a relevant reference point for making sense of American racial (and racist) realities. These analogies were not only taken to be inoffensive to most American Jews; they were widely understood to reflect common sense. It was a double standard, many felt, for the United States *not* to turn its full attention to the eradication of white racism at home after German fascism had been defeated abroad.

The Cold War

With the rise of the Cold War, nearly every element of American society endorsed the anti-communist consensus. In prior years, many liberals (along with leftists and left-wing sympathizers) had proclaimed American white racism and German Nazism comparable evils. By 1949, this analogy had virtually vanished – ridiculed as the product of "Communist-fabricated hysteria." Only those few sympathetic to communism continued to press the anti-racist linkage; and they were declared anti-American, because their rhetoric "furnished new grist for the Kremlin propaganda mill" ("The Peekskill Riots" 265). In 1948, New York University philosopher Sidney Hook had already spelled out a new analogy: it was Soviet communism that most resembled Nazism.[3]

Increasing numbers of Jewish commentators suggested that Jews made the best and most loyal Cold War Americans precisely because their suffering at the hands of Nazism had taught them to abhor the excesses of totalitarianism. Fear that Jews might be tarred with the anti-communist brush was great. Suspected Jewish communists and communist sympathizers were expelled from every major American-Jewish organization. Many Jews retreated from active roles in left-wing causes.

Analogies between Nazism and American racism grew far less acceptable among Jewish liberals. In general, the American-Jewish community hesitated to align itself too closely with any cause championed on the American left. The vast majority of Jewish intellectuals and leaders retreated wholesale from making pronouncements that could possibly be interpreted as anti-American or pro-communist. Civil rights continued to be

---

[3] Indeed, communism was an even greater threat to democracy than Nazism had been, according to Hook, because American communists weakened the nation from within.

supported, but far more cautiously.

Left-wing interpretations of the Holocaust were again powerfully rejected in 1953 with the controversial case of Ethel and Julius Rosenberg. Indicted on charges that they had conspired to commit espionage, the openly leftist pair persistently denied being communist spies, or plotting to pass classified data about the U.S. nuclear program to the Soviets. The Rosenbergs were convicted and sentenced to death in April 1951, at the height of the Cold War. The Jewish community "as a whole distanced itself from the Rosenberg case" primarily as a way to demonstrate, by its silence, that the Rosenbergs' Jewishness had no bearing on the case (Antler 208).[4]

Still, as Lucy Dawidowicz noted at the time, Ethel Rosenberg invoked the Holocaust in her defense. When her appeal was denied (by a Jewish judge), she reportedly called out: "This is the way the *Judenrat* performed for the Nazis in the Warsaw Ghetto" (Dawidowicz "Rosenberg Case" 44). This Holocaust analogy by a convicted communist spy, however, was not to be trusted. Dawidowicz cautioned that any such charges coming from Ethel Rosenberg or her communist friends were calculated – "intended merely as a trial balloon [to] pick up sympathy and support from individual Jews who may be suckers for this particular bait." Any move to mobilize a "Jewish" campaign to save the Rosenbergs was evidence only of the communist movement's talent for heartless exploitation. (Dawidowicz "Rosenberg Case" 41-42). Liberal commentator and *Commentary* associate editor Robert Warshow also dismissed the Rosenbergs as fake Jews: "since the propaganda built up around the case emphasized the fact that the Rosenbergs were Jewish, they simply adopted the role that was demanded of them"[5] (Warshow 417).

The pro-communist journal *Jewish Life* took a different view: it called the American Jewish Committee (*Commentary's* sponsor) "the agency of the big bourgeoisie." It charged that the

---

4   An international campaign sought to have the death sentences commuted, but President Eisenhower denied a final clemency plea. Ethel and Julius Rosenberg were executed in the electric chair on Friday afternoon, June 19, 1953. Out of respect for their Jewish identification, the executions were rescheduled to precede sunset and the beginning of the Sabbath.

5   Indeed, Warshow continued, "If something else had been needed, they could as easily have taken up the pose of Protestantism or Catholicism or Gandhiism."

"Rosenbergs were killed as an offering to the Cold War," and warned that those responsible for the Rosenbergs' execution were "trying speedily to kill the Bill of Rights, tear the Constitution to shreds and to bring fascism to our country" ("Human Dignity" 3).

Such hyperbolic pronouncements – placing America on the brink of fascism – made any analogy between Nazism and U.S. politics seem completely outrageous. It also thereby made it next to impossible to invoke the Third Reich in discussions of American racism. Over the course of the 1950s, references to Nazi crimes in political discourse dropped off dramatically. It was only toward the late '50s and early '60s that the Holocaust and its relationship to American politics resurfaced. However, it did so in competing and mutually irreconcilable forms.

Bystander Anxiety

On August 28, 1963, at the March on Washington rally, Rabbi Joachim Prinz, president of the American Jewish Congress, gave a brief address titled "The Issue Is Silence." At Prinz's side stood Martin Luther King, Jr., who was to deliver his "I Have a Dream" speech that same afternoon. The crowd that late summer day numbered 200,000. Prinz spoke of his years as a rabbi in pre-war Berlin,[6] an intimate witness to the advance of Nazism. Standing before the Lincoln Memorial, his speech revitalized the link between German anti-Semitism and American racism that had been all but erased during the Cold War. "I speak to you as an American Jew," he began – but in the speech that followed Prinz repeatedly said "we" and "our," indicating a self-consciousness that he spoke for every American Jew. He said:

> As Americans, we share the profound concern of millions of people about the shame and disgrace of inequality and injustice which make a mockery of the

---

[6] Before his expulsion by the Gestapo, Prinz had been (in the words of one Berlin congregant) "something unheard of in Germany of that period – an ardent, devout and militant Zionist [who] resolutely and unflinchingly [spoke out] against the rising tide of National Socialism." Prinz had even "urged the immediate emigration of Jews from Germany to Palestine, unmasked the shallowness of assimilation, and appealed, again and again, for identification of German Jewry with the eternal fountainhead of the Jewish people and with the upbuilding of its ancient homeland" (Nussbaum 5-6).

great American idea.

As Jews, we bring to this great demonstration, in which thousands of us proudly participate, a twofold experience – one of the spirit and one of our history (Prinz 252).

For Jews, he explained, "neighbor [is] a moral concept [that] means our collective responsibility for the preservation of man's dignity and integrity." Jewish history, he continued, told of an ancient heritage of oppression that "began with slavery and the yearning for freedom." American Jews felt "not merely sympathy and compassion for the black people of America, [but] above all [a sense of] complete identification and solidarity born of our own painful historic experience" (252-3). Elaborating on why American Jews struggled for racial justice after Auschwitz, Prinz offered a Holocaust lesson not available in the 1940s:

> When I was the rabbi of the Jewish community in Berlin under the Hitler regime, I learned … that bigotry and hatred are not the most urgent problem. The most urgent, the most disgraceful, the most shameful and the most tragic problem is silence.
>
> A great people which had created a great civilization had become a nation of silent onlookers. They remained silent in the face of hate, in the face of brutality and in the face of mass murder. America must not become a nation of onlookers. America must not remain silent. Not merely black America, but all of America. It must speak up and act, from the President down to the humblest of us, and not for the sake of the Negro, not for the sake of the black community, but for the sake of the image, the idea and the aspiration of America itself (Prinz 252-3).

A rabbi attending the March on Washington told *Hadassah Magazine* that Prinz's speech mirrored his own feelings: "Had this march taken place in the 1930s in Germany, there might never have been the mass murder of Jews. The conscience of the Christians in Germany might have been awakened as our consciences are being awakened today" (Michaels 40).

Prinz had formulated a kind of Holocaust analogizing that might best be called "bystander anxiety." If American Jews failed to put themselves at risk to work on behalf of African Americans, then they would be behaving no better than German citizens had under Nazism.

Bystander anxiety had already begun to find expression in rabbinical and other Jewish circles. In 1958, Rabbi Jacob M. Rothschild of Atlanta had asked, regarding civil rights activism: "How can we condemn the millions who stood by under Hitler, or honor those few who chose to live by their ideals, when we refuse to make a similar choice now that the dilemma is our own?" (Greene 189). In 1962, in an indicative turn of phrase, gentiles who had rescued Jews from the Holocaust were honored as "Freedom Riders" ("The Embattled Minority" 4). A year later, Rabbi Richard Rubenstein, describing a discussion at the convention of the Conservative movement's Rabbinical Assembly (concerning the proposed establishment of an institute "to document altruistic deeds done by non-Jews to save Jews during the Hitler holocaust"), reported the following exchange:

> The proposal touched an understandably sore nerve. In the midst of the debate, one rabbi queried why we were concentrating our energies on what had happened twenty years ago [during the Holocaust].... Then, almost as an afterthought, the rabbi asked whether the Rabbinical Assembly was doing the right thing by meeting together rather than adjourning to Birmingham, Alabama, to aid Dr. Martin Luther King and his followers in their struggle for human rights (Rubenstein "Rabbis" 5).

These were far from isolated cases. Increasingly, rabbis who saw social-justice concerns as integral to their faith found, in the Holocaust, a reference point underscoring the moral righteousness of anti-racist activism. The years 1963-64 would witness the full flourishing of this line of argumentation. It was no concidence that a high percentage of those young Northeners who went south to assist in African American voter registration drives and Freedom Summer were Jewish.

Such a political interpretation of the Holocaust's lessons remains alive in the early 21st century, especially in liberal-left Jewish circles. It did not, however, go unchallenged.

Jewish Survival

A competing (and implicitly less liberal) political expression of Holocaust consciousness came to prominence also in the early 1960s. It stressed the urgent need for American Jews to focus on their own communal survival. Interestingly, this opposite perspective was also formulated in the context of civil rights activism.

At the start of the 1960s, a number of prominent American-Jewish leaders expressed irritation at the community's ardent involvement in civil rights and liberal causes. In 1960, Milton Himmelfarb accused the American Jewish Congress of being more concerned with civil rights than with Jewish religion, education or culture. That same year, *Midstream* editor Shlomo Katz wondered aloud whether civil rights activism wasn't simply a fad wherein students engaged in cathartic, social guilt-releasing bouts of group therapy. Protesting segregation seemed just to be a "fashion" and a "salve for the conscience" (Katz 33). Also that year, both Himmelfarb and the new *Commentary* editor, Norman Podhoretz, accused American-Jewish liberals of inadequate consciousness about the enormity of the Nazi genocide. Meanwhile, Rabbi Emil Fackenheim lamented the inability of young Jews to express what was repugnant about Nazism; he proclaimed "liberal Judaism ... a contradiction in terms" (Fackenheim 30).

In 1963 and 1964, the attacks on liberal and radical Jews became more fervent. In his now-famous essay, "My Negro Problem – And Ours," Podhoretz confessed to "twisted feelings about Negroes." But he also expressed annoyance at white liberals who, in his view, "romanticize Negroes and pander to them [or] who lend themselves ... to cunning and contemptuous exploitation by Negroes they employ or try to befriend." Podhoretz expressed condescension towards African Americans even as he also invoked Auschwitz:

> Did the Jews have to survive so that 6 million innocent people should one day be burned in the ovens at Auschwitz? It is a terrible question and no one, not God himself, could ever answer it to my satisfaction. And when I think about the Negroes in America and about the image of integration as a state in which the Negroes would take their rightful place as another of the protected minorities in a pluralistic society, I wonder whether they really believe in their hearts that such a state can actually be attained, and if so *why* they should wish to survive as a distinct group. I think I know why the Jews once wished to survive (though I am less certain as to why we still do): they not only believed that God had given them no choice, but they were tied to a memory of past glory and a dream of imminent redemption. What does the American Negro have that might correspond to this? His past is a stigma, his color is a stigma, and his vision of the future is the hope of erasing the stigma by making color irrelevant, by making it disappear as a fact of consciousness (Podhoretz "My Negro Problem" 98-101).

Less iconoclastically, but with similar effect, an increasing number of Jewish commentators argued that Holocaust consciousness should cause Jews to withdraw from involvement in civil rights activism and/or criticized African Americans and black culture.

They also began to make the argument that Jews who stayed involved in civil rights activism were self-hating. In seeking to revise the proper meaning of Holocaust consciousness, for example, Abraham G. Duker[7] attacked Jewish civil rights activists. Speaking at a conference on black-Jewish relations, Duker acknowledged the legitimacy "of this intensive interest in the Negro struggle on the part of so many Jews.... [It] stems from the Jewish tradition of social justice (usually called 'prophetic' tradition)." However, Duker stressed the necessity of taking into account the consequences of such interest – for "in many cases Jewish communal involvement in integration [has come] at the cost of neglecting ... Jewish survival." Blacks were turning on Jews, Duker suggested, because of their own "disappointments with the pace of integration." The Jewish community's very survival was at risk, he said, if Jews did not recognize how black "demands on [them] are sometimes veiled with threats [and] are remindful of prolegomena to quotas, robberies, confiscations and pogroms"[8] (Duker 20-9).

Warning that "genocidal Negro extremists have been given respectability and recognition," he analogized: "That is what happened to anti-Semites in Germany, and the world is still paying for it." Duker was no less harsh on Jews advocating the rights of blacks, calling this a "masochistic approach to their own people." Through an extended chain of associations, he brought together Holocaust imagery with Jewish involvement in civil rights:

> The gas chambers and crematoria have proved at least to one generation the bankruptcy of assimilation in Europe. Nevertheless, the pressures of acculturation, Jewish deculturation and thereby de-Judaization have been increasing, with hedonism and deracination as their most visible hallmarks. Departure from the community through intermarriage and indifference follows.... In the United States escapism from Jewishness has also found expression in the integrationist movement. I know of cases of escapist identification of Jews with the integration struggle to

---

[7] Duker was an editor of *Jewish Social Studies* and a professor of history at Yeshiva University.
[8] He also compared demands for the "Negroization" of Harlem stores to German "Aryanization" propaganda.

the extent of extreme *jüdischer Selbsthass*[9] and active anti-Semitism.... (Duker 20-9).

Marie Syrkin, editor of the *Jewish Frontier*, offered another influential example of this new Holocaust consciousness coupled with disdain for blacks. In "Can Minorities Oppose 'De Facto' Segregation?" Syrkin gave several reasons why a civil rights push for desegregation "is not only self-depreciating but deflects energy from more meaningful demands." She made explicit reference to her post-Holocaust Jewish identity in the essay:

> Any point of view which runs counter in any significant respect to the current Negro civil rights program is bound to be suspect. For this reason I preface my comments with the statement that I am impelled to write not as a white liberal, though I believe the label fits, but as a member of a minority which knows more about systematic discrimination and violent persecution than any group in history. In the immediate as well as historic experience of Jews, a ghetto is not a metaphor; it is a concrete entity with walls, stormtroopers and no exit save the gas chamber. And wherever Jews have lived, varying gradations of bias and social exclusion have been their daily diet. I offer these credentials to indicate Jewish expertise in what it means to be a suffering minority. However brilliant his individual success, Auschwitz is in the consciousness of the modern Jew, reinforcing historic memories of catastrophe.

Syrkin warned that black activists should not pursue strategies likely to result in the "resentment of groups formerly in agreement with Negro goals." Careful not to advocate or prescribe civil rights policy, Syrkin claimed only to document actual events and real obstacles facing the struggle for racial equality. Her analogies and examples, nonetheless, revealed a wholly negative view of

---

[9] In German, "Jewish self-hate."

integration efforts. Calling for full integration, she wrote, amounted to a societal *reductio ad absurdum*. She likened it to "discover[ing] that most of my fellow passengers on some bus routes or subway trains happened to be Jews. Would I then be justified in protesting *de facto* segregation on my bus?" No more, she concluded, than she should "be expected to travel to Harlem in the interests of integrated dining" (Syrkin 6-9, 11-12).

Syrkin also introduced the theme of self-hate in her essay. History, she claimed, had taught the Jewish people how a minority survives. "Self-respecting" Jews knew survival could – and should – mean a desirable degree of voluntary communal separateness. Only "self-hating Jews" would ever view *de facto* segregation of the Jewish community "as oppressive.... Except for avowed assimilationists, Jews have never made complete integration a goal"[10] (Syrkin 7, 9-10).

In the course of this argument, she articulated negative stereotypes of African Americans: school integration, in her view, had already proven itself a failure. Black children transferred into formerly all-white schools just "found themselves in the majority in 'slow' classes." Teachers could hardly be expected "to abandon academic standards" (Syrkin 10-11).[11] Statements about black educational levels or even blacks' purported cultural pathology would become even more common in the course of the mid-1960s.

A subsequent exchange of views about black-Jewish relations printed in *Midstream* in 1966 included more such comments. Leslie Fiedler contrasted the Jewish community's "commitment to a life of logos ... the whole Gutenberg bit" with the black community's existence in "the world of sub-literacy, unrationalized impulse, and free fantasy" (Fiedler 23-25). That same *Midstream* symposium included Lucy Dawidowicz's comparison of African-American militancy and Nazism.[12] It was "hard to distinguish Black Power from Black Shirts," she observed. Furthermore,

---

[10] Syrkin pointedly asked: "A minority may justly oppose the quality of housing, schooling or job opportunities available to it, but with what grace can it object to a preponderance of its own people?"

[11] Of the several responses to Syrkin printed in *Jewish Frontier*, only one commentator, Reform Rabbi Balfour Brickner, challenged her assumption of African-American inferiority.

[12] Akin to Duker's analogy between "Negroization" and "Aryanization."

Jews involved in Students for a Democratic Society, Student Nonviolent Coordinating Committee and the Congress of Racial Equality were "alienated" from their own heritage, "spitting in the wells from which they drank" (Dawidowicz 13-17).

A new set of associations and arguments was evolving. Blacks were not like Jews; blacks, especially when militant, were like Nazis. Jews who worked on behalf of blacks were self-hating and seeking to escape their Jewishness. And the Holocaust's lesson was that Jewish survival should be paramount. Jews who continued to adhere to liberalism, the new theory went, must not be very proud of their heritage. This cluster of beliefs was in dramatic contrast with earlier interpretations of Holocaust consciousness, which had urged Jews to identify with other oppressed minorities and refuse to be bystanders to injustice.

This trend did not go uncontested. Shad Polier and Justine Wise Polier, for instance, challenged Podhoretz directly in an essay titled "Fear Turned To Hatred." Podhoretz had mocked masochistic whites "who romanticize Negroes and pander to them." The Poliers called the *Commentary* editor's vision of Jewishness "woefully insensitive" to the broader context of black lives and "suffused with self-pity" and "infantile self-appreciation."

> One cannot but wonder whether the doubt later expressed by Podhoretz concerning the value of Jewish survival does not stem from a preference, conscious or unconscious, to be part of the powerful white *goyim* who could oppress, rather than to be part of any minority which might suffer oppression" (Poliers, 5-7).

Was it Podhoretz, the Poliers implied, who might really be the self-hating Jew? They were particularly aghast at Podhoretz's invocation of "the ovens of Auschwitz" for the purposes of criticizing black efforts to survive as a group. With these remarks, "the writer reveals his own moral bankruptcy," the Poliers said. "The concept of loving oneself not in terms of narcissism but in terms of self-respect and the ideal of loving one's neighbor and the stranger, the great themes of Judeo-Christian ethics, are to be cast aside," they accused. Seeing in Podhoretz's writing an "admission of self-contempt," the Poliers concluded it was precisely the "great heritage" of commitment to the ideal of "human brotherhood [that had] made the survival of the Jewish people meaningful to Jews as men, and to those lands in which the Jews have lived" (Poliers 5-7).

Tensions grew in the years that followed, when not just Jewish liberalism but the very meaning of Jewish survival would become the subject of overt and extended controversy. The Six Day War between Israel and the Arab nations marked a turning point in American-Jewish politics. But as the intense debates over U.S. race relations so decisively show, this seeming turning point of 1967 also needs to be understood as the culmination of an extended conflict that had been brewing for quite some time. Within the United States, the Israeli victory over the Arab nations in 1967 consolidated agendas and arguments whose foundations had long ago been laid. In the wake of Israel's victory, these ongoing debates only became more combative.

Jewish Pride

Many American Jews interpreted the Six Day War as a second potential Holocaust; some even viewed Israel's victory as divinely ordained. Even those put off by a religious interpretation felt something profoundly redemptive about the war's outcome. Podhoretz wrote of the tremendous catharsis felt by most American Jews after the Six Day War, which would "reinforce a thousand fold a new determination we had already tasted as a saving sweetener to the bitter sensation of isolation and vulnerability." The emotional American-Jewish response to Israel's military victory, he added, "represented the recovery, after a long and uncertain convalescence, of the Jewish remnant from the grievous and nearly fatal psychic and spiritual wounds it [had] suffered at the hands of the Nazis" (Podhoretz, "A Certain Anxiety" 6).

Dawidowicz summarized the dominant post-Six Day War mood as "a new kind of pride in being Jewish, in the aura that radiated from General Moshe Dayan, his ruggedness, vigor, determination. Many Jews took pride in the changed image of the Jew, no longer seen as victim or the historic typification of a persecuted people." American Jews, whose strongest political identification had been with the civil rights and anti-Vietnam War movements, "discovered the importance of being Jewish" (Dawidowicz "American Public Opinion" 205). Indicative of this ardent newfound Jewish pride – and its links to the Holocaust – was the following letter to the *Village Voice:*

> I think it must have been this way for many of my generation, that the Israeli-Arab collision was a moment of truth. For the first time in my grown-up life, I really understood what an enemy was. For the first time, I knew what it was to be us against the killers.
>
> Us. Two weeks ago, Israel was they; now Israel is we. I will not intellectualize it.... I will never kid myself that we are only the things we choose to be. Roots count.
>
> And I will never again claim to be a pacifist; I will never again say that, if I had been an adult during World War II, I might have been for non-intervention, or, if a man, been a conscientious objector. I have lost the purity of the un-tested... (Dawidowicz "American Public Opinion" 211).

Certainly some American Jews continued to voice dissenting perspectives. In the immediate aftermath of the Six Day War, for instance, left-wing commentator I.F. Stone observed that "Israel's swift and brilliant military victory only makes its reconciliation with the Arabs more urgent." He called upon the world Jewish community, which had undertaken a "huge financial effort to aid Israel" in a time of war, now to use those funds for "a constructive and human cause." This meant that Israel should, Stone wrote, "find new homes for the Arab refugees, some within Israel, some outside it, all with compensation for their lost lands and properties."

It was a moral tragedy – to which no Jew worthy of our best Prophetic tradition could be insensitive – that a kindred people was made homeless in the task of finding new homes for the remnants of the Hitler holocaust. Now is the time to right that wrong, to show magnanimity in victory, and to lay the foundations of a new order in the Middle East in which Israeli and Arab can live in peace.... The first step toward reconciliation is to recognize that Arab bitterness has real and deep roots. The refugees lost their farms, their villages, their offices, their cities and their country. It is human to prefer not to look at the truth, but only in facing the problem in all its three dimensional frightful reality is there any hope of solving it without new tragedy (Stone 1-2).

Yet Stone's interpretation of the Six Day War – especially his reading of the Holocaust and its lessons – was not widely shared. The new commitment to Jewish pride and Jewish power gained momentum from diverse quarters.

Radical Zionist youth, inspired by and in emulation of Black Power, argued that proper Holocaust consciousness meant identifying with Israel as a Third World nation. In rejecting their parents' assimilationist strategies, and turning against "Bagels & Lox Judaism," the younger generation also overtly acknowledged the psychic damage caused by anti-Semitism. They labeled Jewish establishment leaders "Uncle Jakes" (a nod to black militants, who referred to their more accommodationist elders as "Uncle Toms"); they launched dozens of campus journals dedicated to exploring Jewish identity; they demanded, through protest actions, far more attention to Jewish education within the United States; and they urged American Jews to make *aliyah*[13] (and did so themselves). Cartoonist Jerry (now Yaakov) Kirschen joked about it in his strip: "Calling All Zionists: Will all the ZIONISTS please stand up? WRONG! 'Cause if you're still here in Amerika [sic]

---

[13] In Hebrew, "rising." Common term for diaspora Jews' resettling in Israel.

... you ain't no Zionist! ... you're a shmuck" (Kirschen 7).

Jewish Power

According to a poll taken in the late 1960s, one in four American Jews supported the militant Jewish Defense League. Another survey by the American Jewish Congress found one in three of that moderate group's membership supported Rabbi Meir Kahane's right-wing organization.

Kahane made the Jewish capacity for self-defense central to his message. He urged each Jewish man to stop being a "Nice Irving." (Klein Halevi 79). He warned Jews to stop being "patsies" (*Jewish Defense League* 275). In "A Small Voice," Kahane's regular column for the Brooklyn-based Orthodox *Jewish Press,* he wrote:

> Vandals attack a Yeshiva – let that Yeshiva attack the vandals. Should a gang bloody a Jew, let a Jewish group go looking for the gang. This is the way of pride – not evil pride, but the pride of nation, of kinship.... There are those who will protest: This is not the Jewish way. And yet since when has it been a *mitzvah* to be punished and beaten? Since when is it a *kiddush hashem*[14]....? It is not a *kiddush hashem*, it is quite the opposite. It is a disgrace to the pride of our people, our G-d. (Kahane 36)

Kahane's philosophy blamed an inability to confront the legacy of the Holocaust for all the Jewish community's problems. The spiritual sickness of American-Jewish identity lay precisely in a reflexive inability to defend itself against aggression, according to JDL and other radical Zionist thinking. Along with the slogan "Never Again," JDL advocated that all Jews learn martial arts and that all Jewish children join rifle associations.[15]

The Holocaust was a prominent part of JDL's message. It figured centrally in the group's most controversial recruitment

---

[14] From Hebrew, respectively, "blessing, good deed"; "sanctification of the Name (God)."
[15] Through its "Every Jew a .22" campaign, JDL offered, for a nominal fee, a rifle together with a *siddur* (prayerbook) and *yarmulka* (skull cap) to any Jew requesting it (Staub 227).

tool: a large *New York Times* advertisement that appeared in June 1969. Prompted by SNCC leader James Forman's decision to read aloud a demand for reparations for slavery at the city's leading white Christian churches and at Temple Emanu-El, the ad showed several JDL toughs, armed with baseball bats and lead pipes, gathering to defend the synagogue.[16] The ad's caption asked: "Is This Any Way for Nice Jewish Boys to Behave?" The answer followed:

> Maybe. Maybe there are times when there is no other way to get across to the extremist that the Jew is not quite the patsy some think he is.
> Maybe there is only one way to get across a clear response to people who threaten seizure of synagogues and extortion of money. Maybe nice Jewish boys do not always get through to people who threaten to carry teachers out in pine boxes and to burn down merchants' stores.
> Maybe some people and organizations are too nice. Maybe in times of crisis Jewish boys should not be that nice. Maybe – just maybe – nice people build their road to Auschwitz (31).

In this way, the JDL resuscitated the popular and profoundly problematic theory that Jews had been passive under Nazi persecution. Indeed, one of the most striking aspects of Holocaust consciousness in the late 1960s and early '70s was the exacerbation, rather than the rejection, of the myth that Jews in Europe's ghettos and death camps had gone "like lambs to the slaughter." This stereotype[17] was eloquently refuted in the course of the 1960s by Podhoretz, Alexander Donat and others. Jewish power advocates chose, however, to reinforce the "passive Jew" myth at this moment to advance their cause both in Israel and the United States.

---

[16] Forman never showed up.
[17] Strongly endorsed in Bruno Bettelheim's *The Informed Heart* (1960) and Hannah Arendt's *Eichmann in Jerusalem* (1963).

Rabbi Richard Rubenstein's public declarations of the utter necessity of embracing Jewish power took on special significance, for he spoke both as a former civil rights activist and a leading post-Holocaust theologian. By the late 1960s, Rubenstein had articulated an openly macho interpretation of Holocaust consciousness. He considered it a chronic misinterpretation to regard anti-Semitism as something belonging to "the category of emotional abnormality." He argued that "there may be something altogether predictable and even normal about the antipathy often expressed towards Jews" (Rubenstein "Imperatives" 33-34). To place anti-Semitism on the shelf with abnormality was to minimize how it continued to saturate the world, something Jews did at their own great peril. Only Zionists, Rubenstein told a conference in Rehovoth, Israel, had correctly understood anti-Semitism – and had responded to it by seeking to create a Jewish national homeland.

One consequence of Jewish nationhood was that Jews had to learn new skills and deploy new methods to defend their state.

> In a word, the re-entry of the Jewish community into the realms of nationhood and territory meant a re-entry into the domain of the intelligent use of violence. For two thousand years, the Jewish community had been the passive recipient of aggression. Immense transformations were required in order that the Jewish community attempt to survive in the world of naked power and violence. Secular society's messianic promise had failed. It was succeeded by tribal nationalism to some degree everywhere in the world (Rubenstein "Imperatives" xx).

Without power, especially in a world that respected little else, Jews emasculated themselves. The "realities of naked power" were phenomena that Israelis recognized all too well, Rubenstein noted. Sadly, Jews in the Diaspora, imbued with a self-destructive "Jewish messianic optimism," had come to consider powerlessness itself as "a special virtue." But to accept a self-abnegating view toward power "after the gas chambers" was a risk of tremendous proportions:

> After the European Holocaust, the entailments of powerlessness should have proven so degrading and frightening that no Jews with a measure of inner dignity would ever want to be placed in that position again. Powerlessness can mean that the lives and the honor of one's women, one's children and one's person are subject to the good graces of others. Faith in the continuous virtue of men, at least in the ways in which they confront Jews, seems hardly justified by recent history. We do not wish to suggest that imminent danger now threatens the American-Jewish community. We merely suggest that its inability to comprehend the question of power is rendered problematic by recent Jewish experience (Rubenstein "Imperatives" 37).

Rabbi Steven Schwarzschild drew a different lesson from the Holocaust. A refugee from Nazism himself, Schwarzschild felt Rubenstein's perspective defamed the memory of Holocaust victims. "That's not security," he said. "That's insecurity. That's not self-assertiveness and pride in one's identity; that's pathology" (Schwarzschild "Discussion" 40). Entering the realm of statehood and power, Schwarzschild opined, seemed to be accompanied by a disturbing "transvaluation of all Jewish values."

"The problem of our Jewish generation and of our children," Schwarzschild said, "is whether we can live with the ethics and politics of the persecuted, having, in some ways, ceased to be the persecuted. I implore you and me and all of us not to prove Nietzsche to have been right – that morality is the rationalization of the weak" (Schwarzschild "Jewish Survival" 2-21). Schwarzschild insisted that he was "as committed as anybody on earth to the sanctity of every inch of the Holy Land." But he was disturbed to find Jews starting to behave like "men of the new Fascism [rather than] the men of spirit that the Jewish people have always been." To Schwarzschild, Zionism "has to do not so much with survival as with the opportunity to test and incarnate Jewish values on the soil of Israel" (Schwarzschild "Discussion" 41).

However, the space for combining a commitment to Israel's safety with left-wing causes was narrowing. Critiques of Israeli militarism became unacceptable in the American-Jewish community and were met with immediate rebuke. Increasingly, also in the domestic context, during the 1970s concern about the biological survival of Jews began to displace earlier debates about the content of Jewish values. For example, Bill Novak, editor of the Jewish countercultural journal *Response*, in 1971 expressed both the overarching trends of the time and his own hesitations about those trends when he stated:

> Several years ago, during the civil rights movement, there were those who said disdainfully, 'nobody helped us' and 'let them pull themselves up by their bootstraps like we did.' These reckless comparisons are being repeated now in new forms, as if we must give the world tit for tat, as if there were no special obligations, no sense of destiny, or of mission, that Jews have always possessed. And as long as we are here, it is our duty to make life in America better for all people; and this needn't be at the expense of ourselves. For we must assert it loudly: Mere existence, for Jews, *even in the wake of Hitler*, is simply not enough (Novak 309).

Population Panic

In the course of the 1970s, one further wrinkle entered the debate over what lessons American Jews should draw from the Holocaust. Much tension within the Jewish community focused, at this time, on the future prospects of the Jewish family and the supposed need for Jewish women to have more babies. A corollary to this new argument asserted that the most appropriate response to the Holocaust was to challenge and oppose aspects of the sexual revolution.

Some Orthodox leaders did not hesitate to invoke the

Holocaust in making a case against abortion. Among the most influential was Rabbi Walter S. Wurzburger, first vice president of the Rabbinical Council of America. In 1973, speaking at a conference sponsored by the Federation of Jewish Philanthropies of New York, Wurzburger opined that "having lost one-third of our population in the Holocaust and lacking sufficient population to settle the land of Israel, the Jewish community does not reproduce itself adequately" (19). By early 1976, he expressly condemned Reform leaders' pro-choice stance as "insensitive to the injurious effects on Jewish survival which permissive abortion represents." He added:

> It is particularly reprehensible for Jewish groups to promote abortion in light of the fact that the Jews have not yet replaced the Holocaust losses and in light of the fact that Israel needs more population desperately and yet has an alarming rate of abortion ("Rabbi Denounces Jews" 2).

Nevertheless, most American Jews continued to support birth control and abortion rights and to embrace many aspects of the sexual revolution. A broadening range of advocates, both male and female, from across the denominations expressed vocal dismay that Jewish women were not heeding the call for more children. Jewish leaders counseled families to have four children or more; to do otherwise would be to risk allowing Hitler a posthumous victory. In 1971, a Reform rabbi told the *Jewish Post and Opinion* that up to the year 2000, "each Jewish family should have at least four children." If Jewish families had only two children, he calculated, the community would, in effect, be "fixing our numbers at the level established by Adolf Hitler" ("Rabbi Recommends 4-Children Family" 3).

In 1974, Rabbi Sol Roth, president of the New York Board of Rabbis, identified the low American-Jewish birth rate of the previous three decades as a "Holocaust-size loss." While he declined to take a position on "zero population growth for the rest of the human family," Roth said he firmly believed that "three

children should be the minimum number for Jewish families...
but the larger the better" (Spiegel 40). Also in 1974, an essay in
Reconstructionist – titled "Are the Jews Committing Jewish
Genocide?" – argued that the "all-time low" fertility rate, among
Jews, while "not the result of local pogroms, massive
extermination campaigns by Nazis or Communists, or even
intermarriage, [could have the same] ultimate effects [as these]
within only one or two generations" (Roberts 37).

In 1975, Rabbi Norman Lamm, president of Yeshiva
University, noted that although world population control was a
"moral imperative," the Jewish situation required special
consideration. "Jews are a disappearing species," he argued, "and
should be treated no worse than the kangaroo and the bald eagle."
Lamm recommended that each married Jewish woman have four
or five children ("The Disappearing Jews" 39). Even the typically
liberal-minded Central Conference of American Rabbis (Reform)
released a statement after its annual convention in 1977 urging
Jewish families "to have at least two or three children" because
"there are simply not enough of us to be assured of survival in
succeeding generations" (Frank 13).

One of the few to examine critically the strategies of pro-
fertility advocates was *Lilith* contributor Shirley Frank. In her
1977 critique of the Jewish fertility debates, Frank quoted from a
1961 *Commentary* article by Milton Himmelfarb. He had posed
the following moral dilemma: "Where does a Jew's obligation
lie? Should he absent himself from paternity awhile, for the good
of the human race? Or should he be of good courage, and play
the man for the people?" One wonders, Frank noted archly, "what
'play the man' means in this context. It seems clear, however,
that the man is making decisions about his paternity quite as if he
were a self-fertilizing flower." Challenging rhetoric that constantly
associated "the present downward trend in population growth ...
with the Holocaust – as if those who are failing to reproduce in
sufficient numbers are somehow collaborating with Hitler," Frank
also countered:

> The fact remains that we cannot replace the Holocaust
> victims, and any attempt to equate the unborn with Jews

who were murdered is an insult to the martyrs' memories – for surely we define those 6 million Jewish lives in terms more significant than their numbers alone. Moreover, those who urge women to breed more babies for the sake of increasing the Jewish population are strangely, indeed, shockingly, echoing Hitler's exhortation of German women to breed more babies for the Fatherland (Frank 15-6).

In earlier years neo-conservative intellectuals (such as Nathan Glazer and Robert Alter) had castigated Jewish liberals and leftists for applying the term "genocide" too loosely to the abusive treatment of African Americans. Now Frank was at pains to point out that Jewish pro-fertility activists were themselves using the term very loosely and using it with "abandon to describe what we are supposedly doing to ourselves" (Frank 14). It was not by chance, Frank thought, that the campaign to raise Jewish numbers gained momentum just as the community felt the first tentative stirrings of a Jewish feminist movement. Could it really be only coincidence, she wondered, that as Jewish women began to demand a greater role in both communal and religious life, a chorus of men were "loudly hitting the old 'barefoot-and-pregnant' motif as if our very lives depended on it?"[18] (Frank 16-17).

Rejecting Victimhood

In the decades since the 1970s, there has been at least one further major development in the evolution of Holocaust consciousness and its relationship to American political culture. Interestingly, it represents a dramatic reversal of attitudes. In the 1960s and '70s, many formerly liberal American Jews sought to redefine their political views through a stronger identification with the victims of the Holocaust; the 1980s and '90s, however, witnessed a move away from such redefinitions. Indeed, historian Edward Shapiro noted a significant backlash against "American Jews'

---

[18] The pro-fertility rhetoric "depresses and disgusts me," Frank concluded, "not so much because I am a feminist, but because I am a Jew. I am deeply ashamed at the idea of Judaism sinking to a level where we are scrounging around for every warm body we can get."

image of themselves as impotent victims" (433). Indeed, for Shapiro, "the sense of the Jew as victim helps explain why radical Jews support other groups also perceived to be victims – such as Palestinians, grape pickers and garment workers in Central America" (Shapiro 431).

It was an interesting turnabout. In the 1960s and '70s, liberal and leftist Jews had been accused of insensitivity to the lessons of the Holocaust; two decades later, they were taken to task for an obliviousness to "the joys of Jewishness" precisely because they focused so intently on the Holocaust (Shapiro 432).

"One of the challenges facing American Jewry," Shapiro writes in 1998, citing Alan Dershowitz: "… 'is to move the Jewish state of mind beyond its past obsession with victimization, pain and problems and point it in a new, more positive direction, capable of thriving in an open society'" (435).

Today, the perceived problem with progressive Jews is that they have too *much* rather than too *little* Holocaust consciousness. Perhaps unsurprisingly, Shapiro is disdainful of Jewish feminists' fighting for abortion rights, and identifies the low Jewish birthrate and intermarriage rates as the great moral challenges facing American Jews. His essay – and it is symptomatic of much wider trends – constitutes an unabashed call on Jews to drop their old commitments to liberalism and civil liberties and to bring their politics more in line with their rising economic and social status.

Conclusion

Recent reports suggest that an intensification of the longstanding rightward drift is indeed occurring. Throughout the 1980s and '90s, American-Jewish commentators delighted in repeating the old Milton Himmelfarb axiom: Jews have the social status of Episcopalians, but they vote like Puerto Ricans. Yet the *Jerusalem Post* in 2002 reported "it's an open secret that presidential advisor Karl Rove sees the Jewish vote as critical to [George W. Bush's] reelection chances in 2004" ("The Jewish Vote"). A recent study by sociologist Steven M. Cohen made an equally dramatic claim: "American Jews may be poised on the edge of a historic shift to the right in their political views," he reported in the *Forward*, and "younger Jews are far more willing than their elders to identify as Republicans and to approve of President Bush" (Cohen).

In this newly configured political landscape, references to the Holocaust have certainly not disappeared, and continue to be used to make political points about the evolving present. In an article[19] on President Bush's visit to Auschwitz during a one-day trip to Poland in June 2003, the *New York Times* reported that although "never one to linger at sightseeing," Bush nonetheless "took in the camps, the barracks, the gas chambers and the scenes of torture in about an hour and a half." And subsequently, the president inscribed in the Auschwitz guest book the words: "Never forget." Still, reporters traveling with the president's entourage were informed that this tour of Auschwitz had "a diplomatic" purpose – a "searing indictment of modern France and Germany," because those nations refused to join the American-led coalition against Saddam Hussein in Iraq. As the article noted, the message of statements by both Bush and national security advisor Condoleeza Rice was that parallels between Hussein and Hitler "were obvious," and that those nations which had failed to back the U.S. invasion of Iraq had "made a huge historical mistake" (Sanger 14).

What we are seeing in the present, then, is a mix and match of contradictory gestures. When Holocaust consciousness would seem to advance a conservative agenda, conservatives (both Jews and non-Jews) embrace it. When Holocaust consciousness would seem to impede such an agenda, they reject it. At the same time, those who see different lessons in Nazism, who worry about the consequences of "preemptive war," the erosion of civil liberties, or the dismantling of international institutions are energetically rebuffed.[20] Most importantly, the loss of historical knowledge about the complex earlier American-Jewish debates over the potential lessons of the Holocaust has serious consequences in the present. In particular, it significantly constrains the ability of younger generations of American Jews to imagine a passionate and serious debate over what could and should constitute Jewish values for the future.

---

[19] Under the headline "Witness to Auschwitz Evil, Bush Draws a Lesson."

[20] For example, see *New York Times* staff writer James Traub's recent harsh criticism of what he called "Weimar Whiners" (Traub 11).

POLITICS   139

Works Cited

Abrams, Charles. "Homes for Aryans Only." *Commentary* 3 (May 1947): 421.

Antler, Joyce. "A Bond of Sisterhood: Ethel Rosenberg, Molly Goldberg and Radical Jewish Women of the 1950s." *Secret Agents: The Rosenberg Case, McCarthyism, and Fifties America.* Eds. Marjorie Garber and Rebecca L. Walkowitz. New York: Routledge, 1995.

Cahnman, Werner J. "Race Riots in the Schools." *Jewish Frontier* (November 1945).

Cohen, Felix S. "Alaska's Nuremberg Laws." *Commentary* 6 (August 1948).

Cohen, Steven M. "Survey Sees Historic Shift to the Right." *Forward* 17 January 2003 <http://www.forward.com/issues/2003/03.01.17/news1.html>.

Dawidowicz, Lucy S. "American Public Opinion." *American Jewish Year Book 1968.* Eds. Morris Fine and Milton Himmelfarb. New York: American Jewish Committee, 1968. 198-229.

—. "'Anti-Semitism' and the Rosenberg Case." *Commentary* 14 (July 1952).

—. "Negro-Jewish Relations in America: A Symposium." Contribution. *Midstream* 12 (December 1966): 13-17.

"The Disappearing Jews," *Time* 14 July 1975: 39.

Duker, Abraham G. "On Negro-Jewish Relations - A Contribution to a Discussion." *Jewish Social Studies* 27 (January 1965): 20-29.

"The Embattled Minority." Editorial. *Reconstructionist* 28 (June 2, 1962): 4.

Fackenheim, Emil L. "The Dilemma of Liberal Judaism." *Commentary* 30 (October 1960): 301-310.

Fiedler, Leslie. "Negro-Jewish Relations in America: A Symposium." Contribution. *Midstream* 12 (December 1966): 23-25.

Frank, Shirley. "The Population Panic." *Lilith* 1 (Fall-Winter 1977/78): 12-17.

Glazer, Nathan. "Blacks, Jews and the Intellectuals." *Commentary* 47 (April 1969): 33-39.

—. "Jewish Interests and the New Left." *Midstream* 17 (January 1971): 32-37.

Greene, Melissa Fay. *The Temple Bombing*. Reading, MA: Addison-Wesley, 1996.

Hentoff, Nat. "Introduction." *Black Anti-Semitism and Jewish Racism*. Ed. Nat Hentoff. New York: Richard W. Baron, 1969.

Himmelfarb, Milton. "In the Community." *Commentary* 30 (August 1960): 158-9.

"Is This Any Way for Nice Jewish Boys to Behave?" Advertisement. *New York Times* 24 June 1969: 31.

The Jewish Defense League: Principles and Philosophies. New York: Education Department of the Jewish Defense League, n.d.

"The Jewish Vote." *Jerusalem Post* 5 November 2002.

Kahane, Meir. "A Small Voice." *Jewish Press* 26 July 1968: 36.

Katz, Shlomo. "Notes in Midstream: Negroes and We." *Midstream* 6 (Spring 1960): 31-33.

Kirschen, Jerry. "And Now… The Pig City Follies." *Hakahal* 1 (March-April 1972): 7.

Klein Halevi, Yossi. *Memoirs of a Jewish Extremist: An American Story*. Boston: Little, Brown, 1995.

Michaels, Ruth Gruber. "March on Washington: The Enemy is Silence." *Hadassah Magazine* 44 (September 1963): 40

Novak, Bill. "The Failure of Jewish Radicalism." *Jewish Radicalism: A Selected Anthology*. Eds. Jack Nusan Porter and Peter Dreier. New York: Grove Press, 1973. 305-309.

Novick, Peter. *The Holocaust in American Life*. Boston: Houghton Mifflin, 1999.

Nussbaum, Max. "Dr. Prinz at 60." *Congress Weekly* 29 (June 25, 1962): 5-6.

"The Peekskill Riots." Editorial. *Crisis* 56 (October 1949): 265.

Pfeffer, Leo. "Defenses Against Group Defamation." *Jewish Frontier* 13 (February 1946).

Podhoretz, Norman. "A Certain Anxiety." *Commentary* 52 (August 1971): 6.

—. "My Negro Problem – and Ours." *Commentary* 35 (February 1963): 93-101.

Polier, Justine Wise, and Shad Polier. "Fear Turned to Hatred." *Congress Bi-Weekly* 30 (February 18, 1963): 5-7.

Prinz, Joachim. "The Issue is Silence." *The Dynamics of Emancipation: The Jew in the Modern Age.* Ed. Nahum N. Glatzer. Boston: Beacon Press, 1965. 252-3.

"Rabbi Denounces Jews Who Misstate Judaism's 'Abhorrence of Abortion.'" *Jewish Week* 29 January-4 February 1976: 2.

"Rabbi Recommends 4-Children Family." *Jewish Post and Opinion* 19 February 1971: 3.

"Radical Students Plan New Confrontation," *Jewish Post and Opinion* 22 May 1970: 3.

Riz, Yaakov. "Breira Rabbis Should Be Asked to Resign or Be Thrown Out." Letter. *Jewish Post and Opinion* 20 December 1974: 5.

Roberts, H. J. "Are the Jews Committing Jewish Genocide?" *Jewish Digest* 20 (March 1975): 37-42.

Rubenstein, Richard L. "Imperatives of Survival." *Congress Bi-Weekly* 36 (February 24, 1969): 31-39.

—. "The Rabbis Visit Birmingham." *Reconstructionist* 29 (May 31, 1963): 4-7.

Sanger, David E. "Witness to Auschwitz Evil, Bush Draws a Lesson." *New York Times* 1 June 2003, 14.

Schoenfeld, Gabriel. "Death Camps As Kitsch." *New York Times* 18 March 1999, A25.

Schwarzschild, Steven S. "Discussion." *Congress Bi-Weekly* 36 (February 24, 1969): 39-42.

—. "On the Theology of Jewish Survival." *CCAR Journal* 63 (October 1968): 2-21.

Shapiro, Edward S. "Liberal Politics and American Jewish Identity." *Judaism* 47 (Fall 1988): 425-436.

Spiegel, Irving. "Rabbi Deplores Small Families." *New York Times* 24 January 1974: 40.

Staub, Michael E. *Torn at the Roots: The Crisis of Jewish Liberalism in Postwar America.* New York: Columbia University Press, 2002.

Stone, I.F. "The Harder Battle and the Nobler Victory." *I.F. Stone's Weekly* 15 (June 12, 1967): 1-2.

Syrkin, Marie. "Can Minorities Oppose 'De Facto' Segregation?" *Jewish Frontier* 31 (September 1964): 6-12.

Traub, James. "Weimar Whiners." *New York Times Magazine* 1 June 2003: 11.

Walters, Joel. "Community Forum." *Cleveland Jewish News* 5 May 1972: 20.

Warshow, Robert. "The 'Idealism' of Julius and Ethel Rosenberg." *Commentary* 16 (November 1953): 413-418.

Wechsler, James A. and Nancy F. "The Road Ahead for Civil Rights." *Commentary* 6 (October 1948): 304.

Wurzburger, Walter S. "Not Rated as 'Necessary Evil,' but 'Swinging Society' is Out!" *Jewish Week and American Examiner* 7-13 June 1973: 19.

Chapter Five

EDUCATION:

Jewish Learning, Jewish Lives: Reflections on the Contemporary American-Jewish Experience

By Meredith Woocher

During the last two decades, interest and attendance in programs of adult Jewish learning has soared, bringing many Jewish adults into serious engagement with Jewish texts and learning for the first time in their lives. In theory, life-long learning has always been a central part of Jewish culture, from Biblical times forward. The Torah, after all, commands the Israelites to not only teach "these words, which I command thee this day" to children, but also to "talk of them when thou sittest in thy house, and when thou walkest by the way, and when thou liest down, and when thou risest up" (Deut. 7:6-7). Throughout our lives, the words of Torah are never to be far from our lips and thoughts.

In reality, however, the importance placed upon adult education has waxed and waned throughout Jewish history

(Goldman 5). The recent resurgence in interest, therefore, is both a hearkening back to previous eras, and a phenomenon particular to today. It is nurtured by such contemporary trends as the increased wealth, security and leisure time of American Jews, the accompanying hunger for spirituality and deeper meaning felt by many in modern society, and the newfound religious opportunities open to Jewish women, who – in contrast to previous centuries – comprise the majority of today's adult Jewish learners.

One such woman, Evelyn, has lived in the same mid-Atlantic Jewish community for all of her 60-odd years. Born and raised in an urban neighborhood, she followed the Jewish migration to the suburbs – as did the Conservative synagogue she had been affiliated with for decades. Although her level of ritual observance has waxed and waned, her commitment to Judaism and the local Jewish community has been a constant. Evelyn's Jewish life has always revolved around the twin poles of philanthropy and community leadership; her social circle is made up almost entirely of people she met through her work as a lay leader in the local chapter of the Jewish Federation or through her synagogue, many of them also life-long residents of the community.

Naomi, a social worker in her mid-40s, has traveled a very different path – one that might never be expected to cross Evelyn's. Raised in a secular Jewish family in the Northeast she spent much of her adult life moving through diverse religious communities in search of a spiritual home. After exploring Buddhism, Quakerism, Ba'hai, and Ethical Culture, she found herself returning to Judaism – a move she credits to the encouragement of her second husband, a Catholic. Today, she is happily involved both in her Reform synagogue and her husband's church – each of which is accepting of her interfaith marriage and her daughter's lesbian lifestyle. What Naomi seeks from her religious affiliation is both a deepened connection to God and an outlet for her passionate social-justice activism.

At first glance, these individuals seem to have little in common, other than being Jewish women in 21st-century America. Yet in the fall of 2000, both Evelyn and Naomi found that their religious journeys had led them to exactly the same place for the same reason. They had joined about 30 other Jewish adults in a synagogue library classroom to embark on a two-year program of adult Jewish-learning.

As suggested at the opening of this chapter, Evelyn and Naomi are hardly alone in their quest for learning. A recent study found that one in five Jewish adults had participated in some form of Jewish learning in the past year (Cohen and Davidson, 8). National programs of Jewish learning – such as the Florence Melton Adult Mini-Schools, the Wexner Heritage program and the Me'ah program based in Boston – have expanded dramatically in the last five years, with multiple sites across the United States and around the world.

Despite this evidence that adult Jewish-learning is an increasingly important phenomenon in American Jewish life, little research has been done to answer some obvious questions. Why are Jewish adults from across the religious spectrum increasingly turning to text study as an expression of their Jewish identity? What questions do they bring with them into the classroom? What do they hope to accomplish intellectually, emotionally or spiritually? What is the actual experience of adult Jewish learners? And, finally, what impacts can Jewish learning have on beliefs, behaviors and communal affiliations? In essence, adult Jewish-learning offers a window into the minds and hearts of contemporary American Jews. By exploring why a group of American Jews chooses to engage with the texts of their tradition, and uncovering the impact that engagement can have on their religious lives, we expose some of the questions, concerns, needs and goals at the center of Jewish life today.

The Adult Jewish-Learning Movement

Larger sociological forces have contributed to the growth of adult Jewish-learning over the past 20 years. The reasons are complex and multifaceted. As statistical studies have documented, the material and educational status of American Jews is higher today than at any other time in Jewish history (Fishman, 40). Contemporary American Jews enjoy higher levels of professional achievement, greater wealth and, often, more leisure time to pursue

Jewish education – upon retirement, if not during the working years. Secure in their success and their ethnic identity, they may be feeling freer to explore their religious identity.

As the Jewish community has become more socially accepted and materially secure, it has also entered a new era of spiritual and religious anxiety. Unlike the external threats of the past (such as anti-Semitism and foreign persecution), the primary threats Jews face today are internal – assimilation, acculturation and intermarriage. Educators and professionals have been concerned with these threats almost since the founding of the American-Jewish community. They became especially alarmed, however, after the publication of the 1990 National Jewish Population Survey, which found that the intermarriage rate had reached 52%[1] (Kosmin 20). As organizations everywhere began to discuss the preservation of Jewish culture, a new buzz-word was coined: "Jewish continuity." How much these concerns influence the daily lives of American Jews is unclear. But according to Betsy Dolgin Katz, the debate has begun "to affect behavior. Individuals see Jewish learning as something they can do to contribute to the continuation and vitality of the Jewish people…. There is a growing sense of responsibility for the Jewishness of this generation and the next which is expressed through learning" (Katz 10).

That large numbers of contemporary Jews seek to reconnect with their tradition is supported by the findings of scholars Steven M. Cohen and Arnold Eisen. According to their study, moderately affiliated American Jews in recent decades have turned away from political and organizational forms of Jewish commitment. Fewer American Jews claim a denominational affiliation than in decades past, and their Jewish identities are no longer impelled or shaped by such global issues as support for Israel, memory of the Holocaust or fear of anti-Semitism: "The communal quest for 'sacred survival' that animated many American Jews a generation ago is simply not what motivates the Jews whom we studied" (Cohen and Eisen 16).

---

[1] Some scholars argue that the more accurate figure is closer to 43%.

However, for many of these people, turning away from communal and organizational definitions of Jewish life does not necessarily mean turning away from Judaism. Cohen and Eisen note that as contemporary American Jews move from the political to the personal and from the community to the self, they devote themselves more and more to the search for Jewish identity and Jewish "meaning." In interviews with the researchers, study participants repeatedly expressed "a strong desire to find a sense of direction and ultimate purpose, and the wish to find it largely or entirely in the framework of Jewish practices and beliefs" (Cohen 8). As Jewish institutions and organizations increase opportunities for such inward exploration, American Jews have responded.

And finally, as has often been the case in American-Jewish history, the Jewish experience closely parallels that of general society. In recent decades scholars of American religion have chronicled a resurgence of religious and spiritual activity in general. According to sociologist Robert Wuthnow, in the last 50 years the religious life of most Americans has been transformed from a "spirituality of dwelling" – passive reception of religion rooted in familiar traditions and places – to a "spirituality of seeking," an active search for religious meaning in multiple settings (Wuthnow 7). Wade Clark Roof, another scholar of contemporary American religion, concurs. "Large sectors of the American population today are interested in deepening their spirituality," he writes. "Many who seem to have lost a traditional religious grounding are striving for new and fresh moorings; many with a religious grounding are looking to enrich their lives further...." According to Roof this desire for religious enrichment springs from the "spiritual hunger" many feel in response to a modern lifestyle that "severs connections to place and community, alienates people from their natural environments, separates work and life, [and] dilutes ethical values, all of which makes the need for unifying experience so deeply felt" (Roof 62). This spiritual search has led people both to intensified practice of a single religious tradition and to shopping for spiritual fulfillment in an ever-expanding "spiritual marketplace."

The Jewish religious search may have unique dimensions – including a prevailing desire to seek meaning within Jewish life and tradition rather than in the wider spiritual bazaar. But it accords with the messages gleaned from the wider society and popular culture: that religion is a primary means of living a better, more fulfilling life.

Methodology

To explore the impact of adult Jewish-learning on contemporary American Jews, I became a participant-observer at one Northeastern site of a national adult Jewish-learning program, the Florence Melton Adult-Mini School.[2] Over the course of nine months, I observed more than 100 hours of classes on Jewish theology, history, ritual and ethics. In addition to classroom observations, I did an extensive analysis of the Melton curriculum, and conducted formal interviews with 40 current and former students. My interview sample was fairly representative of the overall student population – largely female, middle-aged or older, married with children, living in a fairly high-income area and identified with Conservative Judaism. However a diversity of other ages, denominational affiliations and Jewish backgrounds were also represented in the classroom.

By and large, these Jewish Americans had indeed reached heights of educational and professional achievement, and material security. At the same time, they shared a sense of something missing in their lives – needs and questions that the religious experiences of childhood and adulthood had left unanswered and unfulfilled.

For some, the needs were largely intellectual – an attempt either to fill in the gaps left by inadequate childhood Jewish

---

[2] A pioneer in the field of adult Jewish education, the Florence Melton Adult Mini-School is an international network of community-based schools offering adults the opportunity to acquire Jewish literacy in an open, trans-denominational, intellectually stimulating learning environment. Founded in 1986 by Jewish education advocate Florence Zacks Melton, these Mini-Schools now operate in 60 cities throughout the United States, Canada, United Kingdom and Australia, attended weekly by roughly 5,500 students. Students enroll in a sequential two-year course developed specifically for adult learners. They meet one day a week throughout the academic year. There are no examinations. The only prerequisite is a commitment to learn. Four text-based courses make up the sequential two-year curriculum written by a team of experts at the Hebrew University's Melton Centre for Jewish Education – the world's largest academic center for Jewish education (Florence Melton).

education, or to build further upon an already strong, but still incomplete, foundation of Jewish knowledge. Others saw their learning in a more practical light, closely tied to Jewish observance. The greater their understanding of Jewish tradition, the more easily they could make educated and informed choices incorporating aspects of the tradition into their lives. Finally, some learners looked to Jewish learning to fulfill the kind of "spiritual hunger" that Roof had described, hoping that engaging with tradition would help in their personal search for God, connection and meaning.

Why They Study

As mentioned above, many students choose to become adult-Jewish learners in order to satisfy intellectual needs and fill the gaps in their Judaic knowledge. Most, with the exception of a few of the older women, had attended Sunday School or Hebrew School, at least in their early childhood. For many, however, this experience had been unsatisfying and uninspiring, yielding little lasting knowledge of Jewish texts or tradition. Going to Hebrew school was simply "what you did," a boring and obligatory ritual of Jewish upbringing. Whatever their reasons – poor pedagogical skills in erstwhile religious teachers, little interest in religion as adolescents, a sexist environment promoting Jewish education for boys only – the Melton students lacked a foundation of Jewish knowledge. But they had come to see adult Jewish-learning as a valuable opportunity to rectify the deficiency.

Even those satisfied with their childhood Jewish education described a hunger for Jewish knowledge, a desire to "just learn," that had brought them into the classroom as adults. Some felt that their level of Jewish knowledge was low enough that it hardly mattered what they were learning, since any amount on any topic would add volumes to their meager store. Stacy, a nurse in her early 40s who had converted to Judaism at age 22, explains that she entered her first adult Jewish-learning class with a completely open and eager mind: "I just really wanted Jewish learning. I had really no expectations other than to come out of there knowing more about being Jewish than I knew when I went in."

Kim, a Jewish educator in her late 20s, had similar thoughts, even though it turns out her level of Jewish knowledge was not as basic as she had believed: "I'm frustrated," she says, "because I feel like I'm working as a Jewish educator and I don't know the things I want to know. The ironic thing is, I got there and I knew a lot more than a lot of other people did." Although they do not explicitly say so, Stacy and Kim may both see Jewish learning as a passport to worlds in which they feel insecure – the Jewish world in general for Stacy, the Jewish professional world for Kim. They are, perhaps, content to "just learn" any and all subjects because it is the act of learning, rather than any specific knowledge they gain, that helps them to feel more comfortable in their Jewish identities.

Finally, many students report feeling keenly the contrast between the high level of intellectual skill and competency in their secular and professional lives, and the minimal skills and knowledge they bring to their Jewish lives. With their religious training either non-existent, greatly lacking, lost in the fog of memory or frozen at a 13-year-old level, they wish to bring their Jewish education in line with their far-richer secular education. Develop a more complete and systematic understanding of Judaism, they know, will not advance them professionally. But it will enable them to re-examine their religion though the eyes of an adult, rather than those of a teenager.

At the other end of the spectrum, there are students who framed their learning goals as a spiritual search, or a quest for meaning. In articulating their goals and questions, these students reveal a great deal about how they define "spirituality." Doris, a psychotherapist, speaks eloquently about her own journey: "I had just turned 60 years old, and I realized that my own spirituality was really at a very superficial level, that I was nowhere near as knowledgeable about my own spirituality as I was about the psychological composition of the human brain," she says. "I felt that it was time to sit down and read and hear discussion and be in the company of a community where I would be able to engage, and that would lead me to a deeper sense of spirituality." Through readings and discussions of texts with classmates, Doris says she hopes to develop a roadmap for a higher-level connection to "a power greater than [my]self, to the soul and one's beliefs and values." She is less concerned about the specific texts or ideas of study than about creating a community of learning Jews.

Though Doris alludes to "a power greater than [her]self," like many contemporary American Jews she does not explicitly name this power as God.[3] Other learners, however, use more traditional God-language when discussing their spiritual quests. One describes "turning away from God," when her father had died, turning back after her mother's death, and wanting to include learning as part of that return. Once she had let God back in her life, she explains, "that eventually led to the question of what God required of me. So I felt I should find a way to really learn more about that." Other students identify specific spiritual and theological questions, such as why good people suffer, why God allows evil in the world.

Finally, a few learners don't specifically mention "God" or "spirituality"; they say they look to Jewish learning to counter the superficiality and alienation pervasive in American culture and society. Dora, a retired teacher in her late 70s, contrasts the "meaning" available from Jewish text study with the materialism of contemporary life: "Our lives have gotten so full of material things in America today. You start to feel that it's so meaningless … having your this, having your that. I was just looking for something more in my life … to hang my hat on, to give me greater satisfaction." Similarly Selma, a publisher in her early 60s, is interested in what Jewish study could bring to an alienated society that has "come loose from its roots" and lacks understanding of "God, how to live, ethics, goodness. We don't know about our history."

Together, these learners offer a vivid critique of modern life, in which people are caught up in materialism and largely severed from the teachings of the past. They, along with many of their fellow classmates, are both products and resistors of this culture. Having enjoyed the benefits of secular American society, Dora

---

[3] Cohen and Eisen found that nearly half of their respondents did not describe God as a personal being, but rather "as a force in nature, or in ways consistent with that view" (157).

explains, they are ready to ask: Is that all there is to life? And, if not, how and where can they find more?

Finally, there are learners who combine intellectual and spiritual goals, seeing the search for knowledge as a pathway to increased Jewish meaning. These students look to adult Jewish-learning not only for the "whats" of Jewish practice and history, but also the "whys" – seeking to add meaning to already-familiar Jewish rituals. For adults with young children at home, the desire to "know about the whys" is often tied to a desire to create a Jewish home and to be a better Jewish parent. Roberta frames her quest as a responsibility to her young son: to "be able to answer his questions," to "be a role model to him." Roberta articulates what many Jewish parents feel implicitly: that they must "model" for their children how to lead a Jewish life. She is also reacting against the poor model her own parents had provided: that when it came to Judaism they "didn't know and didn't care." Thus Roberta's desire to study is rooted in three generations of tensions and negotiations surrounding religion – including the doubts and questions she imagines her son will someday face.

Other learners, often those whose children are grown, frame their search as a personal quest for greater confidence or fulfillment. Paula, a child-care professional in her early 60s, seeks coherent explanations for all of the details of observance she had absorbed in her life: "I've got all this trivia stored up," she says. "Everybody's got all this trivia – I think it's just what happens as you go through life. I wanted some explanations. I know that there aren't explanations for everything. But I did want to know about the whys and where-it-came-froms [to get] that in-depth meaning."[4]

Even as they seek out the meanings and explanations behind Jewish practice, none of the students express the sense that understanding would necessarily lead to observance, or inspire them to more traditional practice of Judaism. Rather, explains Sandra, a physician in her late 30s, adult Jewish-learning expands

---

[4]   In referring to the pieces of Jewish knowledge and rules for practice she had accumulated as "trivia," Paula is not suggesting they are trivial or unimportant. A desire to learn more about this "trivia" is what had driven her to the adult Jewish-learning classroom.

the options for observance by helping one make more informed choices about religious belief and practice. "I want the information so I can make decisions about what I think and what I don't think," she says. Gaining knowledge allows her to make choices, and the act of choosing is itself, for Sandra, an expression of Judaism.

Finally there are students who, in seemingly contradictory fashion, say they hope learning will bring them both definitive answers about how to live a meaningful Jewish life, *and* the knowledge to make educated, independent, choices. Michelle, a teacher in her mid-30s, talks at length about her quest for answers and the freedom to question. On the one hand, she explains, "I like to be given answers. I am not the kind of student who likes to search them out on my own." At the same time, Michelle believes once she has gained answers through study, she will be able to identify her own Judaism and question it. "Even if I got to the point where I was doing Shabbat every Friday night and coming to services every Saturday, I would still question."

If Michelle's goals for her religious life sound a bit confused and ambivalent, they are an accurate reflection of the tensions and uncertainties many contemporary Jews experience. She, like many American Jews, feels a conflicting need for both authority and autonomy.

Knowing why American Jews choose to engage in adult Jewish-learning, we now turn to the question: What do they get out of the experience? What insights and answers do they take from the texts they study, and what impact do these ancient and classical texts have on their thoroughly modern, American lives?

Sociologists often divide religious life into three primary spheres of activity: believing, behaving and belonging. In thinking about the impact of Jewish learning on Jewish lives, this triad serves as a useful organizing framework. "Believing" encompasses all of the attitudes and insights learners expressed about God, Torah, tradition and authority. "Behaving" describes not only actual Jewish practices and observances, but also the meanings and interpretations learners attach to those practices. And "belonging" refers less to institutional affiliations than to the sense of connection learners develop toward their local communities, religious denominations and the Jewish people as a whole. In actuality, of course, these categories constantly overlap and interact: one can hardly talk about Jewish practice or communal affiliations without addressing underlying beliefs.

Believing

As we saw above, many students come to Jewish learning seeking answers to troubling theological questions. Roberta, who hoped to "make sense of her own questions" about certain Jewish prayers and images of God, describes her perceptions changing as a result of insights she gained from her teachers and fellow learners. For example, the High Holiday liturgy that asks "Who shall live and who shall die" had formerly made Roberta "angry or upset"; through close study, she has come to understand that "you don't necessarily take [these prayers] literally … you can be consumed by inner torment, or things like that." With this new, metaphoric reading, Roberta was able to "swallow" a previously unpalatable dimension of Jewish theology.

Patty, a homemaker in her mid-50s, offers a similar comment. The course has not changed her "personal belief" or "image of God," she says. Yet it has given her "a different view of the role that God can play in your life." For Patty, as well, the moment of insight is tied to new interpretations of previously troubling language: "I've always wondered why you say "fear" God. It's not really to fear God but to be in awe of God. That makes much more sense to me, because I wouldn't want to believe in a God that we have to fear." Both Patty and Roberta came away reassured about dimensions of Judaism that had disturbed them, and convinced that their relationship to God and prayer is stronger because of it.

In addition to investigating their relationship with God, learners also question and probe traditional religious concepts – such as the authorship of the Torah. Their conclusions are often ambiguous as adult learners try to reconcile and incorporate contradictory theologies and negotiate conflicting beliefs and practices. Kim, for instance, talks about her struggle to come to terms with "the whole revelation thing," the metaphysical implications of her belief or disbelief, and the notion of "truth" as applied to the words of Torah. She often thinks "these are just stories people created to help them understand the world." But she also recognizes that the act of interpreting the world through narrative lends the stories their own "truth," even if it is not literal truth: "The validity is in the story and the way we use it to shape our lives. [When] my students ... say to me, 'Kim, is that story true?' I feel very comfortable saying, 'I don't know if it happened exactly this way, but it is true.'"

Recognizing that belief functions on multiple levels, Kim describes the struggle between head and heart, between her rational disbelief in divine revelation and her emotional desire to believe "because it gives me comfort." She eases the tension between these two doctrines by finding a third approach in which the concept of "truth" is a flexible one. The Torah has a "deeper truth," dependent not on its historicity but on the "way we use it to shape our lives," she says. One's focus should not be on the events of the past, but on the meaning we give it in the present. What Kim seems to be describing is her sense of Torah as the central "informing myth" of Judaism and the Jewish people, a tale that is the source of values and identity, rather than historical data. Because Torah is, for Kim, not a historical truth but an informing myth, she recognizes that her belief is an active and deliberate one, something she had "chosen...to buy into."

Other students similarly find that their learning helped to bring them to new and more complex understandings of the origins and meaning of Torah. Joyce describes how before becoming an adult-Jewish learner, she had believed that any interpretation other than that the Torah was written word for word by God was Jewishly unacceptable. Since being exposed, through texts and teachers, to the idea that the Torah might have been written by humans over the course of centuries, Joyce feels more comfortable with Jewish theology, and is reaching new levels of sophistication in her religious beliefs. God is no longer a remote and threatening being who might "strike her down" should she stray from traditional views. The teacher's role as an authority that can legitimize her views is crucial. Ultimately, Joyce could break with tradition not because of her own internal confidence, but because "my teacher said it," giving her ideas validity.

On the other hand, Sarah, a teacher in her late 40s and a life-long adherent of Reform Judaism, finds that being exposed to a range of views on revelation solidifies her own liberal theology. She explains, the contrast between her views and traditional beliefs make her feel more secure in her own identity as a non-traditional Jew, one who is "right there with Reform." The theological discussions in the classroom thus not only strengthen her beliefs, but also her sense of belonging to a particular Jewish community. Interestingly, even as Sarah confidently espouses the idea that "man created the Torah," she also, half-jokingly, labels her statement "blasphemy." Though she presumably does not truly believe her ideas to be blasphemous or even problematic – especially given the weight of the liberal Jewish community supporting them – she reveals through her words the lingering influence of traditional ideas even as she overtly rejects them. For many of the learners who discuss revelation, traditional beliefs are not so easily cast aside – as evidenced by Kim's struggle between intellect and emotions, Joyce's fear of being "stuck down" for her statements, and Sarah's lighthearted confession of "blasphemy." Even though many learners explicitly reject the idea of a "God of fear," the imagery of an angry God who might strike someone down for uttering blasphemy is apparently still very much a part of their God concept, emerging during moments of candid and emotional reflection.

Finally, many people describe the opportunity to go "back to the sources" as among the most meaningful dimensions of their studies; this alone reflects the still-strong pull of Jewish tradition. For Paula – the learner who hopes to fit the "trivia" she had absorbed into a meaningful context – the original texts offer everything from rationales behind traditions she had long practiced to support for certain political positions: "It's been really important to me to see where things are in the text," she says. "Like on *kashrut*[5] and

---

[5]   Jewish dietary laws.

about eating meat and milk; I can see that we have a reason for it. And when we learned about Israel. I mean, we need to show the Arabs we are right here in this book that was handed to us thousands of years ago – that the land does belong to us." Sandra also speaks of the importance of learning about the "original" biblical teachings, so she could engage in her own process of interpretation: "You hear rules about *kashrut* and people interpret it from A to Z. But what did the Torah actually say? All this other stuff I think is people's interpretation…. I'm getting back to the original so that I can really figure out for myself what it means." By drawing a distinction between the "original sources" and "people's interpretations," Sandra is able to grant equal validity to her own interpretations, which are no less related to the sources than those of rabbinic tradition. In this way, she is able to ground her Jewishness in the authority and authenticity of Jewish text and tradition, yet still maintain the autonomy and freedom of choice that shape the religious worldview of contemporary American Jews (Cohen and Eisen 8).

Behaving

With a few exceptions, learners don't report changes in Jewish practice or behavior. Rarely is there a dramatic increase in synagogue attendance, observance of *kashrut* or Shabbat rest. A number of learners, however, describe significant changes in their emotional connection to or intellectual understanding of behaviors that were already part of their lives, such as prayer and holiday observance. They use words like "confidence," "ease," and "meaning" to explain their new relationship to Judaism and Jewish practice. Joyce, who talks about the greater theological "comfort" that her learning brought, also says she has developed greater "ease" in her ability to participate in synagogue services, though, outwardly, her behavior has changed little. After years of feeling "upset" at services because she could not understand the Hebrew of the prayer book, she now feels "relaxed" in synagogue, and "at such peace with Judaism."

Debra, a researcher in her early 30s, also talks about feeling greater assurance in her Jewish practice and identity. Familiarity, in this case, breeds not contempt, but confidence. "Having to actually go back and read the Bible and read the Torah and the Prophets gives me much more familiarity.... That's what helps me personally build confidence. Knowing where I'm at." Although they don't articulate it in these terms, both Joyce and Debra experience a deeper interaction between study and practice. Familiarity with and understanding of the texts is meaningful, but so is finding a context for them outside the classroom. The insights drawn from their lessons have particular emotional impact for these learners – two of the more traditional in their practice, if not necessarily in their beliefs – because they can be absorbed into a Jewishly committed environment.

Paula explicitly makes this point in her reflections. Learning, she says, has helped her "pull together" pieces of her Jewish life that were already there, but had lacked a framework to give them meaning: "I'm finding that things that I say each week at *shul*[6], about which I didn't know a whole heck of a lot, have been explained to me.... Sometimes things get to be rote when you do them all the time. I'm now more conscious of what I'm saying. More conscious of where I am."[7] Although many students focus on the prayer service, others mention other rituals or celebrations. Patty, for instance, describes how learning makes her "more aware of all the holidays," and how her Passover *seder* (ritual meal), in particular, allows her to explore new dimensions of her knowledge: "We've always had interesting discussions around the table but now I was a little more knowledgeable historically of what went on. I was able, because of what I'm learning, to participate more. Not to be afraid to open my mouth." Patty's concluding thought – "I've always done these [rituals] but not always known the reasons" – sums up the experience of many learners.

---

[6] Synagogue.
[7] Interestingly Debra and Paula use nearly the same phrase to describe how learning has influenced their observance. (Compare Debra's "know where I'm at" and Paula's "more conscious of where I am.") On a literal level, Debra may have meant that she can now more easily find her place in a *siddur* (prayerbook), and Paula, that her mind is more focused on her surroundings in the synagogue. But their choice of words may have symbolic significance as well. They do not say that text study has helped them discover "who" they are, suggesting that their personal and religious identity was never in question. Rather, learning has helped them locate their familiar selves in new contexts – spatial (within the synagogue), communal (within their congregation), historical (within Jewish tradition) and even cosmic (within a divine universe).

Finally, Stacy, a Jew-by-choice, finds the greatest impact of her studies not on her ritual life (which, in the years since her conversion, has become increasingly traditional), but on her perspective toward ethical behavior. Good deeds, such as visiting the sick or burying the dead, had before seemed "just ordinary acts that you did," she says. "I never really associated holiness with them." Once exposed to the Jewish values and texts informing these behaviors, however, she could see them as holy acts, or *mitzvot*.[8] Stacy's emphasis on ethics might make her experience seem less "Jewish" than that of learners focusing on rituals. It is unlikely she conceives of *mitzvot* in the traditional sense, as commandments given by God. But she is one of the few learners to point to the link between human ethics and "holiness," however defined. Her insights could thus be seen as particularly bold, especially since she was raised Catholic and didn't encounter Judaism until her early 20s.

A few of the learners beginning at a low level of ritual observance report experiencing dramatic changes in their Jewish practices. Often, these people cite other Jewish decisions or contexts surrounding their experience in the classroom. For Tammy, a stay-at-home mother in her early 30s, initiation into Jewish learning dovetailed with the decision to enroll her daughter Jenny in a Jewish day school. "Together, the two experiences led to increased home observance in the family. "As each holiday came," she says, "and as we were learning about it in Melton and Jenny was studying it in school, it just became a richer celebration in the home." Tammy's experience is testimony to the potential impact of "family learning" – multi-generational, Jewish education – on the Jewish life and dynamics within a household. Even though mother and daughter were not literally sharing a classroom, their simultaneous learning allowed her Jewish world to expand on multiple fronts. Tammy characterizes it as "all the pieces coming together." Both dimensions – Tammy's personal "inspiration" and her desire to reinforce Jenny's lessons – together

---

[8] An example of the "moralist" tendencies that sociologist Marshall Sklare identifies as a defining feature of modern Jewish life. In his classic "Lakeville" study of suburban, middle-class American Jews, Sklare defined moralism as the idea that "religious man is distinguished not by his observance of rituals, but rather by the scrupulousness of his ethical behavior." (Sklare 89).

form the foundation for Jewish learning to have a significant effect on Jewish life at home, creating a "richer" and more observant environment.

Naomi also finds herself increasing Shabbat and holiday observance since becoming an adult Jewish learner. Like Tammy, she credits both Melton and family influences, although of a very different order. Naomi receives encouragement from her Catholic husband, who is himself deeply interested in the Jewish roots of his own faith. Although he remains a committed Christian, attending church weekly (with Naomi at his side) and celebrating Christian holidays, Rick is equally enthusiastic about incorporating the Jewish rituals into their home practice.[9] This would suggest that multiple religious contexts – and not necessarily only Jewish ones – might fruitfully interact with Jewish learning and lead to positive outcomes (by Jewish communal standards).

Belonging

As with Jewish behavior, most of the effects of learning on Jewish communal ties are internal and subtle – revealed through students' feelings of connectedness rather than any significant change in their institutional affiliations. The sense of "belonging" is expressed in widening circles of connection: from one's place within the local community, to one's ties to a particular denomination; to one's link with the entire Jewish people and their history.

For some, it is the mere act of study, rather than the content of those studies, that weaves a connection to fellow learners and the larger local Jewish community. This is particularly true for recent arrivals. Being part of a learning community is helping Robin, a high-school English teacher in her late 30s, feel more at home in a new city. Not only has the Melton program allowed her to meet

---

[9] Naomi's experience adds an interesting wrinkle to the conventional wisdom on intermarriage and Jewish involvement. A non-Jewish partner is often assumed by many Jews to be, at best, a neutral figure who presents no barrier to Jewish engagement. Here, not only is her Christian husband a significant factor in motivating Naomi to increase her Jewish observance; it was *his* Christian identity that encourages them both to explore and engage with Judaism. This religious dynamic is certainly made less complicated by the fact that Naomi and her husband (a second marriage) have no children at home.

new neighbors and make new friends. Her classmates and their stories have become part of the learning experience: "I learned a lot about the city listening to the life stories of all of these people," she says. Robin regards her classmates as "living texts" who can offer unique insight into the history and tenor of her new community.

The "old-timers" among the learners also see links between the intellectual and communal dimensions of learning. Joan speaks about the convergence of individual spiritual and intellectual needs, and the social forces and dynamics that helped Melton take root in her community in the first place. Learning had entered the community at the "right time" to address these needs, she notes, referring to its popularity among what she calls the "country club and golf set, who lent the program a certain cache: "I definitely think it's been spread through word of mouth, and it's the right word, from the right mouth." The ability of this in-crowd to help spark a wave of Jewish learning suggests that the community is indeed highly cohesive, such that the "right word from the right mouths" apparently reached many ears.

Meanwhile, Paula reflects upon the appeal of learning to women. "Many of us were not educated very substantially in *Yiddishkeit*[10] ... and I think that's part of the reason a lot of us are taking this course. Women are reaching out universally, looking for some Jewish education." Although the Melton classes, particularly the daytime sessions, are dominated by women, Paula is one of the few to address the needs and histories of American-Jewish women. Her remarks suggest that, for Paula, the learning community is largely about the bonds and experiences Jewish women share. She describes her overall religious community as "thick and tight," but the community of women coming together to overcome their educational limitations is perhaps even tighter, enhancing or even supplanting other communal connections.

Jewish education has an impact on learners' feelings about their denominational affiliations. Some focus on their own denominational identities, clarifying and strengthening ties to a

---

[10] Jewishness.

particular Jewish stream. For others, learning leads to broader insights into the relationships, actual and ideal, between movements. With her life-long commitment to Reform Judaism, Sarah finds that defending Reform beliefs in the classroom is inspiring her to seek more knowledge about and commitment to the movement: "Hearing all the Orthodox viewpoints has just made me become so delighted with the fact that I am Reform.... I just love that it has taken me there – that [learning] has made me become Reform, not because my parents were, but because I really believe that's where I want to be." Sarah's studies are helping her become a committed Jew, making active and knowledgeable choices – an ideal the Reform movement calls for but many of its adherents fail to achieve. In expressing delight with her newfound commitment to Reform Judaism, Sarah uses language at the very heart of the denomination, describing herself as a "Reform Jew by choice," embracing the movement not out of habit, but because "I really believe that's where I want to be." Interestingly, exposure to "Orthodox viewpoints" – not to the principles of Reform Judaism – solidifies Sarah's embrace of her own movement. She finds herself experiencing, in microcosm, what the original Reform leaders had centuries before, when the constraints of Orthodoxy inspired a new Judaism defined largely by what it chose to reject. (Meyer 61).

For Joyce, exposure to contrasting viewpoints clarifies and reaffirms her own Conservative identity and commitment, while helping her to become less judgmental about other movements and their adherents. Even after her studies, Joyce shows little sophistication in characterizing major theological differences: Orthodox Jews are committed to following the laws in, as she puts it, all their "little, tiny" details, while Reform Jews hardly follow any. Nevertheless, Joyce emerges more accepting of the two poles of Jewish observance. Though convinced that she "belongs in Conservatism," Joyce realizes she doesn't "have to compare [herself] to what others do, or judge them for it." Like many Americans and American Jews, Joyce embraces the doctrine of non-judgmentalism ("I'm OK, you're OK") pervading contemporary religious and moral thought.

Other learners echo Joyce's conclusions about denomination and freedom of choice. Michael's learning – unlike Sarah's and Joyce's – hasn't altered his commitment to or feelings about his own denominational identity. But it has increased his respect for others' choices and affiliations: "I came out of [the classes] really thinking that everyone should be able to believe what they want to believe and need to believe. I think it has nothing to do with observance, really, but it has to do with respect for all the denominations of Judaism."

While Michael, a physician in his late fifties, doesn't define "it," he seems to be referring to definitions of authenticity within specific denominations and Judaism as a whole. The lesson he takes from the classroom is that respect for an individual's or another movement's beliefs is a greater test of Jewish authenticity than traditional observance. By extension, the primary responsibility of denominations and their adherents is not to promote their own beliefs and requirements, but to respect the beliefs of others.

Finally, there are those for whom learning augments the sense of "belonging" at the broadest level, strengthening connections to Judaism and the Jewish people. In describing the most significant dimensions of his studies, Sam – a retired organizational consultant in his late sixties – is one of the only learners to cite Jewish history. These lessons, he explains, give a new perspective on his people, his family history and his own Jewish identity. Studying interactions with non-Jewish cultures provides a "sociological understanding" of Jewishness, he says, based on the "tenuousness of Jewish existence" through the centuries. The central question for Sam is: "How have we survived?" While the Melton curriculum covers both triumphs and tragedies of Jewish history, clearly the latter have the biggest impact on Sam. On a more personal level, he can now envision his own ancestors participating in historical events: "Learning about the pogroms, and knowing that my grandfather and other relatives came originally from the Ukraine and Kiev…. It helped give me a sense of the journey they've taken." The lessons from Jewish history lead to even more immediate and personal reflections, prompting Sam to ask: "Where do I fit in? Where do I want to be?" Studying Jewish history provides more questions than answers about Sam's Jewish identity, but, he implies, it also sets his own life within the context of Jewish peoplehood. Questions about his place in the world seemed to have a very personal focus: he asks them with an awareness of a Jewish history and people beyond his own experience.

Patty, rather than looking to the events of Jewish history, finds her Jewish identity strengthened by a minor clash with a non-Jewish organization in her community. When her neighborhood "Welcome Wagon" schedules an event on Rosh Hashanah, Patty, a long-time member, can speak up for her religious needs with confidence and pride: "I've become more self-confident about my Judaism," she says.... "I don't have to hide and skirt around things like that anymore." Patty might have challenged her fellow Welcome Wagon members with or without Jewish learning, but having "knowledge behind" her ideals strengthened her confidence to speak as a representative of the Jewish community demanding sensitivity to Jewish needs.

While Patty's negotiations over meeting times may not have had the same weight and consequences as the pogroms Sam describes, it is interesting that for both, confrontation (actual or hypothetical) with the surrounding, non-Jewish culture brings their own Jewish identity into greater focus. Under threat, the ability to freely express their Jewishness gains value and emotional depth. The experiences of Sam and Joyce suggest that the phenomenon of Jewish identification increasing due to real or perceived threat[11] has not been erased by the years of nearly unprecedented acceptance and success that Jews have experienced in America.

Implications for American Judaism

As we have seen, American Jews choose to engage in adult Jewish-learning for many reasons, and the effects of this learning on their lives are complex and multifaceted, reflecting the diversity

---

[11] Whether in the form of overt and even violent anti-Semitism, or a more subtle social stigmatism that suggests Jews are less than welcome.

of student experiences. Yet within these students' stories a number of common themes emerge; these, in turn, reflect some of the central realities and forces shaping contemporary American-Jewish life. We have seen that Jews are drawn to learning out of a sense that their previous Jewish education and experience have left them feeling incomplete. They sense gaps in their knowledge, spirituality or both, and they seek to fill these gaps through exposure to Jewish texts. When they succeed, as many do, these learners emerge with a newfound feeling of competence and confidence when it comes to Jewish life and practice. One student, Joyce, articulated this sense of comfort and assurance again and again – a newfound confidence in her ability to pray, her interpretations of Jewish texts, and her right to stand up for Jewish causes. After engaging with Jewish texts, several learners say they know "where I'm at." Text study does not impact *who* they are: personal and religious identity was never in question. Rather, learning helps students take these selves and locate them in new contexts – spatial (within the synagogue or Jewish home), communal (within a congregation or larger community), historical (within Jewish tradition) and cosmic (within a divine universe). With continued study, the contexts become increasingly comfortable and familiar.

However, even as students begin to feel more at home in new Jewish contexts or communities, the questions they ask and the answers they find are ultimately deeply personal, reflecting the individualistic nature of modern culture. Robert Bellah and his co-researchers described the individualistic cultural and social patterns of contemporary America in their classic sociological study, *Habits of the Heart: Individualism and Commitment in American Life*:

> Individualism lies at the very core of American culture.... We believe in the dignity, indeed the sacredness, of the individual. Anything that would violate our right to think for ourselves, judge for ourselves, make our own decisions, live our lives as we see fit, is not only morally wrong, it is sacrilegious" (Bellah 142).

Jewish learning is, of course, a long way from the "Sheilaism" that Bellah famously described – in which a respondent claimed to adhere only to her own personal, eponymous faith (Bellah 221). Still, these adult learners are clearly comfortable selecting the aspects of traditional belief and practice that most resonate with them, and constructing from these a Jewish life that's personally meaningful and comfortable. Even the exposure to traditional texts positing another worldview – one steeped in commandment, tradition and communal responsibility – does not fundamentally change this individualistic perspective.

In part because of the importance they place on personal meaning and individual freedom of choice, these adult learners are comfortable living with contradictions and ambiguities, especially in their beliefs about God and Torah. They can believe the Torah is a form of "truth" without feeling the need to change their behavior to accord with Jewish laws derived from Torah. Similarly, the learners draw distinctions that don't necessarily exist in the tradition – particularly between Biblical texts, which have a special authority and authenticity; and later "interpretations," which don't. The act of learning, offering newfound skills in to develop their own opinions and insights about Jewish texts, allows students to add their theological interpretations to the chain of interpretation stretching back to the Torah.

Thus, contemporary Jews can satisfy their desire for both authority and autonomy by creating a Jewish life grounded in and tied to the tradition. Yet they can also preserve their freedom to choose exactly what, when and how to believe or practice.

American Jews, like Americans of other faiths, are seekers. But what they seek is not a dramatically new identity. None of the students observed and interviewed in this study suddenly embraced tradition, or made radical changes in their Jewish beliefs, behaviors or communal affiliations. Rather, they seek competence and confidence in their ability to lead a Jewish life based in knowledge rather than ignorance. They want to be at home in their tradition, and to gain the tools that will let them construct a personally meaningful Jewish life, without relinquishing personal autonomy and freedom of choice.

Some Jewish leaders may be disappointed that Jewish learning seems not to produce dramatic increases in levels of observance or commitment to traditional Jewish practice. Others, however, recognize that increasing numbers of American Jews entering into serious engagement with traditional texts, and emerging with newfound sense of knowledge and competence, as cause for optimism and encouragement. What the ultimate impact of the adult Jewish-learning movement on American-Jewish life will be is still unknown, and will require research both broader in scope and longer in time-frame to determine. However, the dedication and joy of these students in rediscovering their tradition may be the groundwork for a renewed and revitalized American-Jewish community.

Works Cited

Bellah, Robert, et. al. *Habits of the Heart: Individualism and Commitment in American Life.* New York: Harper & Row, 1986.

Cohen, Steven M. and Arnold M. Eisen, *The Jew Within: Self, Family and Community in America.* Bloomington: Indiana University Press, 2000.

Cohen, Steven M. and Aryeh Davidson, *Adult Jewish Learning in America: Current Patterns and Prospects for Growth.* New York: The Florence G. Heller/JCC Association Research Center, 2001.

Florence Melton Adult Mini School Institute, Hebrew University, Jerusalem. <http://www.fmams.org.il>.

Goldman, Israel M. *Lifelong Learning Among Jews.* New York: Ktav Publishing House, 1975.

Katz, Betsy Dolgin. "Adult Jewish Learning – Ten Years of Returning: 1989-1999." *Agenda:* Jewish Education. Vol. 1/No. 12 (1999): 9-12.

Kosmin, Barry et. al., Highlights of the Council of Jewish Federations National Jewish Population Survey (New York: CJF, 1991)

—. "What We Know about Adult Education." *What We Know About Jewish Education.* Ed. Stuart Kelman. Los Angeles: Torah Aura, 1992.

Meyer, Michael A. Response to Modernity: A History of the Reform Movement in Judaism. Detroit: Wayne State University Press, 1988.

Roof, Wade Clark. *Spiritual Marketplace: Baby Boomers and the Remaking of American Religion.* Princeton: Princeton University Press, 1999.

Sarna, Jonathan D. "American Jewish Education in Historical Perspective." *Journal of Jewish Education.* Vol. 64 No. 1-2 (Winter-Spring 1998): 8-21

—. "The Cyclical History of Adult Jewish Learning in the United States: Peers' Law and Its Implications." *Seymour Fox Festschrift,* forthcoming.

Schuster, Diane, "Adult Development and Jewish Family Education." *First Fruit: A Whizin Anthology of Jewish Family Education.* Eds. Adrianne Bank and Ron Wolfson. Los Angeles: The Whizin Institute, 1998.

—. *Anthology of Jewish Family Education,* Eds. Adrianne Bank and Ron Wolfson, Los Angeles: The Whizin Institute, 1998.

—. "New Lessons for Educators of Jewish Adult Learners." *Agenda: Jewish Education.*New York: JESNA, 1999.

Sklare, Marshall and Joseph Greenbaum. *Jewish Identity on the Suburban Frontier.* Chicago: University of Chicago Press, 1967.

Wuthnow, Robert. *After Heaven: Spirituality in America Since the 1950s.* Berkeley: University of California Press, 1998.

—. *Rediscovering the Sacred: Perspectives on Religion in Contemporary Society.* Grand Rapids: W.B. Eerdmans, c.1992.

Zachary, Lois and James Schwartz. *Adult Jewish Learning: Reshaping the Future.* New York, JESNA:1991.

—. *Adult Jewish Learning Reader.* New York: JESNA, 1993.

About the Contributors

About the Contributors

Barry Glassner

Barry Glassner is the Myron and Marian Casden Director of the Casden Institute for the Study of the Jewish Role in American Life and a professor of Sociology at the University of Southern California. Professor Glassner was chair of the Department of Sociology for six years prior to his directorship. Before coming to USC, he served as chair of Sociology at the University of Connecticut and Syracuse University. Professor Glassner has authored four books and co-authored or edited six books; his research papers have been published in leading scholarly journals.

Diane Krieger

Diane Krieger is senior editor of *USC Trojan Family Magazine*, the alumni magazine of the University of Southern California. A winner of numerous CASE awards for various university publications, she has held previous editorial positions at Tufts University and Johns Hopkins University. She holds a bachelor's degree in English from UCLA and a master's in journalism, with a focus on public relations in higher education, from the University of Maryland, College Park.

Hilary Taub Lachoff

Hilary Taub Lachoff is the Associate Director of the Casden Institute for the Study of the Jewish Role in American Life at the University of Southern California. She has a B.A. from the University of Judaism and an M.A. from Vanderbilt University, both in the field of psychology. Ms. Lachoff has authored, co-authored or edited several training manuals, scholarly works and research papers. Her work has been published in *Science*.

Ted Merwin

Ted Merwin earned a doctorate in Theatre in 2002 from the Graduate Center of the City University of New York. He has taught at Bronx Community College, City College and, for the last three years, at Dickinson College, where he also directs the Hillel chapter in the new Milton B. Asbell Center for Jewish Life. He has published academic articles in *Dance Chronicle*, the *Journal of American Ethnic History* and the recent anthology "*Literature on the Move: Comparing Diasporic Ethnicities in Europe and the Americas.*" He also serves as the chief theatre critic for the *New York Jewish Week*, the largest-circulation Jewish newspaper in the United States.

Adam Rovner

Adam Rovner received his Ph.D. from Indiana University's Department of Comparative Literature. He holds an M.A. in comparative literature from The Hebrew University of Jerusalem and a B.A. in English from Washington University. His articles on various facets of Jewish humor have appeared in the *Jewish Quarterly* and *Jewish Culture and History*.

Michael Staub

Michael Staub is an associate professor of English and American Culture Studies at Bowling Green State University. He has a Ph.D. in American Civilization from Brown University. Professor Staub has authored two books, including *Torn at the Roots: The Crisis of Jewish Liberalism in Postwar America*. He is also the editor of the anthology, *The Jewish 1960s: A Sourcebook*, to be published in late 2004. His articles and reviews on postwar American culture and history have appeared in numerous journals and collections.

Nomi Stolzenberg

Nomi Stolzenberg is the Co-director of the USC Center for Law, History and Culture and Professor of Law at the University of Southern California. Professor Stolzenberg received her J.D. from Harvard in 1987. Before joining the USC law faculty in 1989, she clerked for one year for the Chief Judge of the Third Circuit Court of Appeals. Her work on the subject of law and religion, communitarianism and liberalism, and the paradoxes of liberal tolerance has appeared in various law review articles, as well is in edited volumes, including *Engaging Cultural Differences: The Multicultural Challenge in Liberal Democracies* (eds., Shweder, Minow & Marcus), *The Jewish Political Tradition II: Membership* (eds., Walzer, Lorberbaum & Zohar), and *From Ghetto to Emancipation: Historical & Contemporary Reconsideratons of the Jewish Community* (Myers & Rowe).

Meredith Woocher

Meredith Woocher currently serves as the Director of The Covenant Foundation's Jewish Educator Recruitment/ Retention Initiative. She has a Ph.D. in Contemporary American Jewish sociology from Brandeis University, and a B.A. in American Studies from Yale University. Dr. Woocher has conducted research and authored papers in many areas of Jewish sociology and Jewish education, including the history and sociology of adult Jewish learning, the impact of Israel experiences on the Jewish identity of adolescents and college students, and the origins of the

Jewish counterculture and the Havurah movement. Her work on adult Jewish learning will be published in a forthcoming volume from the Jewish Theological Seminary of America Press.

USC Casden Institute
for the Study of the Jewish Role in American Life

University of Southern California,
Grace Ford Salvatori Hall, Room 304,
Los Angeles, California 90089-1697

www.usc.edu/casdeninstitute